"Whether you're in the  ly looking to jump-start a tir̄ ... ̄ōman is for you. You'll laugh, y ... amazed at the fresh infusion of ... ns offer within the pages of this ... . I can't recommend it highly enough."

"I believe Alice and Steve have written with great discernment and wisdom. Their nonjudgmental, hands-on approach makes the reader feel as if she is sitting across the table from her, being gently coached into a place of hope and truth. I wholeheartedly recommend this book to people in any stage of marriage."

"It is the call of every woman to lean on the Lord and learn to love. Before you walk out, read this book; new life might be only a chapter away. Bravo, Alice Gray and Steve Stephens for tackling a subject that is so prevalent today!"

"A must-read for every married couple to protect their marriage from the 'Walk Out Woman' syndrome."

"I believe this is one of the most important books ever written for women. Dr. Steve Stephens and Alice Gray skillfully identify problems women face in marriage. But more importantly they give brilliant insight and godly wisdom to help women change their behavior. This is a must-have book!"

The Walk Out Woman is practical, heartfelt, and realistic. If you're ever tempted to walk out, you'll find *The Walk Out Woman* is an invaluable guide and friend that offers hope, healing, and gentle correction."

—GARY THOMAS
AUTHOR OF *SACRED MARRIAGE* AND *SACRED PARENTING*

"Finally there is help for the growing number of women who suffer in secret, longing for a marriage they can live with. Dr. Steve Stephens and Alice Gray take a hard look at this painful subject with the gentleness of loving friends, giving much-needed direction and hope. *The Walk Out Woman* will help women live up to the comittments they have made and long to keep."

—GEORGENE RICE
KPDQ RADIO, PORTLAND

"*The Walk Out Woman* by Dr. Steve Stephens and Alice Gray will provide a basketful of ideas for any man who wants to love his wife more deeply—and for any woman who is dying to be loved that way. This is a book full of enlightening and entertaining illustrations, deep and penetrating wisdom, and creative ideas about how to make a marriage significantly better. I recommend it."

—NEIL CLARK WARREN
PSYCHOLOGIST AND FOUNDER, EHARMONY.COM

"What can a wife do when her marriage is dying? Steve and Alice give theologically sound, concretely practical suggestions for women who are looking for hope. Here's a 'help book' that's actually helpful!"

—GERRY BRESHEARS, PHD
PROFESSOR OF THEOLOGY, WESTERN SEMINARY

"These pages are an honest and loving conversation with people who really understand what it's like to be in a hurting marriage. If you're there today and don't know what to do about your future, I highly recommend it."

—HEATHER KOPP
COAUTHOR, *BECAUSE I SAID FOREVER*

the walk out woman

the walk out woman

When Your Heart Is Empty and Your Dreams Are Lost

Dr. Steve Stephens and Alice Gray

Multnomah® Publishers *Sisters, Oregon*

THE WALK OUT WOMAN
published by Multnomah Publishers, Inc.
© 2004 by Alice Gray and Dr. Steve Stephens
International Standard Book Number: 1-59052-267-2

Cover design and image by PixelWorks Studio
Interior typeset by Katherine Lloyd, The DESK

Unless otherwise indicated, Scripture quotations are from:
Holy Bible, New Living Translation © 1996.
Used by permission of Tyndale House Publishers, Inc.
All rights reserved.

Other Scripture quotations are from:
The Holy Bible, New King James Version (NKJV)
© 1984 by Thomas Nelson, Inc.
The Holy Bible, New International Version (NIV)
© 1973, 1984 by International Bible Society,
used by permission of Zondervan Publishing House
New American Standard Bible® (NASB) © 1960, 1977, 1995
by the Lockman Foundation. Used by permission.
The Message © 1993, 1994, 1995, 1996, 2000, 2001, 2002
Used by permission of NavPress Publishing Group

Multnomah is a trademark of Multnomah Publishers, Inc.,
and is registered in the U.S. Patent and Trademark Office.
The colophon is a trademark of Multnomah Publishers, Inc.

Printed in the United States of America

For information:
MULTNOMAH PUBLISHERS, INC.
POST OFFICE BOX 1720 • SISTERS, OREGON 97759

Library of Congress Cataloging-in-Publication Data
Stephens, Steve.
     The walk out woman : when your heart is empty and your dreams are lost /
Steve Stephens and Alice Gray.
          p.cm.
     Includes bibliographical references.
ISBN 1-59052-267-2 (pbk.)
     1. Wives--Religious life.   2. Christian women--Religious life.   3. Marriage--
Religious aspects--Christianity.   4. Marital conflict--Religious aspects--Christianity.
I. Gray, Alice, 1939- II. Title.
     BV4528.15.S74 2004
     248.8'435--dc22

04 05 06 07 08—10 9 8 7 6 5 4 3 2 1

*To the women whose hearts feel empty
and yet still care enough to read this book.*

Contents

A Note to Our Readers

We have used many true stories in this book. Unless we had specific permission from the women involved, we changed the names and altered the circumstances enough to protect their privacy.

A Special Thank You...

To our friends
Anita Crowther, Carol Clifton, Keely Hannon,
Karen Jamison, Nancy Meer, and Marty Williams.

*We appreciate your valuable insights
and thoughtful suggestions.*

To the women who responded to our survey.

Your honest answers touched us deeply.

To our editor, Anne Christian Buchanan.

*When we say you are more than wonderful,
we aren't saying nearly enough.*

To Tami Stephens and Al Gray.

*You gave us daily gifts
of love, encouragement, and prayer.*

To our Lord and Savior, Jesus Christ.

*More than anything, we pray You
will find pleasure in what we have written.*

White Linen and Candlelight

To love someone is to learn the song that is in that person's heart and to sing it to them when they have forgotten.

AUTHOR UNKNOWN

t was a wonderful evening—one of those special dress-up affairs for which even the men took extra time and care getting ready. The women looked radiant in their loveliest dresses, the men distinguished in ties and suits. Soft music mingled with laughter and conversation, while the added touches of candlelight, fresh flowers, and fine china on white linen created a romantic mood.

The occasion was a sweetheart banquet for married couples of all ages—from young newlyweds all the way through those celebrating their golden anniversary years. I (Steve) had been asked to be the keynote speaker.

They called me to the podium while everyone was still busy with lively conversations and delicious desserts. Briefly I wondered if getting their attention would be difficult. But as soon as I announced the topic, "Does Your Wife Know You Love Her?" a hush fell over the group. These couples were focused. They clung to every word.

13

Or at least the *women* clung to every word.

When I started explaining about the dreams and longings a woman has for marriage and how often she feels hurt and disappointed when these longings are unfulfilled, nearly every woman in the audience nodded her head in agreement. And yet most of the men appeared indifferent or skeptical about what I was saying. The look on their faces was clear: *This doesn't have anything to do with me.* I could hardly keep myself from stepping off the platform, confronting each one eyeball-to-eyeball, and saying, "You've got to get this. If you don't, your marriage could be in serious trouble and you don't even know it."

When I finished my talk, people were encouraged to linger for an extended social time. I noticed that the women immediately burst into animated conversation with the other ladies at their tables. After a short time, many of them broke away and walked over and individually thanked me for what I had said. Others pulled me to the side and whispered comments like these:

"My husband hardly notices me anymore."

"I'm dying on the inside and don't know where to turn."

"The only reason I'm staying in my marriage is the children."

"I expected so much more for our marriage."

"He is not the same man I dated."

"I'm at the point where I don't think it's worth the effort anymore."

"Surely God doesn't want me to be this unhappy."

I often heard such comments in my counseling office from women as tears streamed down their cheeks. On this particular evening, however, I was caught off guard by the number of women whose pain was so intense that they risked sharing their hurt in a public place—at an event dedicated to celebrating married love. What surprised me even more was that this function was primarily attended by committed Christian couples, many of them leaders in their churches. Of any group, you would think these couples had the highest potential for great marriages. And yet the surprising response I received from the wives indicated marriages in deep trouble.

Before the evening was over, I looked for opportunities to talk to some of the men on a one-to-one basis. "So, how do you feel about your marriage?" I casually asked. To a man, their response could be summed up with two words: "No problem."

Driving home that night, I kept thinking about the contrasting responses I had observed in the men and women that night. I knew that a banquet was hardly the best place to get a candid response from most men. I also knew that women more naturally pay attention to the pulse of a relationship, while men are typically slower to recognize problems. But I couldn't help feeling that what I had observed that night indicated something much deeper.

Although I have always felt an intense concern for marriages in trouble, that night my concern moved to a deeper level. So many women were hurting and losing hope, while their husbands were not even aware of their pain. And my experience as a counselor told me that this discontentment and disappointment, if ignored, had the potential to destroy all the joy and happiness their marriages once held.

I wish I could say I was wrong about that. But five years after that sweetheart banquet, I had counseled seven of the men who attended that evening. They came to my office and told me through tears that the wives they dearly loved, the women they would do anything for, had walked out on their marriages.

Some had walked away angry; others had done it calmly.

Some had given lengthy explanations; others had refused to talk.

All of them said it was too late for their husbands to do anything to win them back.

Are You Ready to Walk?

If you relate to this story even a little bit, this book is for you. Most specifically, it's for you if you're a woman like those I met at the sweetheart banquet—tired, lonely, angry, disappointed, fed up, and perhaps on the verge of walking out on your own marriage. Because you are the one who is most aware of the problem, we are addressing this book directly to you. But we also hope it can be of help to husbands who are baffled by their wives' apparent unhappiness, or perhaps even for friends and family who would like to help.

My coauthor, Alice Gray, and I are passionate about this topic because we have observed a growing epidemic of women walking away from their marriages. We believe this trend can be reversed—and *must* be reversed. We desperately want you to understand the risk of leaving a marriage unattended. But even more, we want you to realize there is always hope, even when it feels like a marriage is over. Even when you're on the verge of walking out.

You captured each other's hearts before, and you can capture each other's hearts again. With a plan, perseverance, and prayer, we know you can have a marriage of enduring love.

Could it be that wedding rings like other things, are lovelier when scarred?

RUTH BELL GRAHAM[1]

17

Before we start, you might want an idea of who we are. Alice Gray and I have teamed up on several other books before—our most recent is *The Worn Out Woman*. We are an unusual writing team because we live in different states and collaborate mostly by phone. During the past ten months, we've been in contact with more than sixty women who have walked away from their marriages or seriously considered doing so. Because of this, we were both able to contribute real-life stories for each chapter. Often I supplied the main data; then Alice reworked it and added personal touches. A group of six women from varied backgrounds read an early manuscript and gave vital comments and suggestions. In addition, we were privileged to have an extraordinary editor, Anne Christian Buchanan, who filled in the empty places. To say that the book is better because of her input is a huge understatement.

My expertise on the subject of marriage comes from more than two decades of successfully counseling couples as a marriage and family therapist. I also enjoy a wide variety of speaking opportunities and have written three other books on marriage, including *20 Surprisingly Simple Rules and Tools for a Great Marriage*. Tami and I have just celebrated our twentieth wedding anniversary and through the years have worked out many of the principles of this book in the crucible of our own relationship. As Tami will attest, even a family psychologist can sometimes be a clueless male—but even a clueless male can learn to be a more loving husband.

Alice brings the valued viewpoint of a mature Christian woman who has a tender heart for women's issues. She is a respected and popular speaker, and one of her most-requested workshops is on the treasures of marriage. Over the years Alice has offered a listening ear and trusted counsel to women whose marriages were in trouble. And she, too, has lived out these principles in her thirty-seven-year marriage to Al.

It is our deep desire that couples will read this book together. Our experience tells us this may not happen—at least not at first. Because wives are typically more sensitive to signs of relationship trouble, we assume that you are our first readers, and we have addressed this book directly to you. We pray that you will recognize the symptoms and dangers of becoming a walk-out woman and that you will realize that it is not a path to happiness. Opening your heart to your marriage again is indeed a risk, but we believe it's a risk worth taking.

We want to help you understand your husband better and show some ways you can encourage him to listen to your hurts and anger. We want to help you understand more about yourself as well—why you may have started "keeping score" and how you have built a wall around your heart. We'll talk about realistic and unrealistic expectations and the dangers of creating a new fantasy with someone else. We'll also give you strategies for taking care of yourself, getting connected again with your husband, resolving conflict, dealing with anger and loss, remembering the good times, and pressing closer to the Lord.

If you are a husband, we commend you on your courage in picking up this book—and we promise you it won't be an exercise in male-bashing. We are well aware that to the male mind, women can seem infinitely complex and baffling. We know you sometimes feel that you can't do anything right. We pray that this book will help you understand your wife's needs a little better and show you ways you can begin to meet those needs with the power of selfless love.

We want you to fight for your marriage—and we want to reassure you that marriages can thrive again even when dreams seem lost. There are specific things you can do to polish the tarnish off your dreams. Your marriage will never be perfect—no relationship is—but it can be deeply fulfilling. In our work and in our own marriages, we have discovered proven methods for moving toward each other instead of away, for building up instead of tearing down, for finding love instead of losing it.

For any marriage, it's vital to remember that what seems like the end can often be a new beginning. Loss of passion does not equal loss of love. Loss of love does not equal loss of hope. Loss of hope does not mean a relationship should be abandoned.

When troubles first begin, hope is resilient, but it gradually becomes fragile and seems to break. But even when hope seems lost, a tiny strand lingers. We pray you will find that golden strand and hold on tightly, for its powerful allure can help you find the way to become one again.

Something to Try

You can choose just one...

- Look over the list on page 14. Which comment expresses most accurately how you are feeling right now? Is there something you would add?

- How do you think your husband would answer the question, "Does your wife know that you love her?" What would be the reasons for his answer?

- What strand of hope for your marriage keeps you holding on to what you have? What can you do to strengthen this strand?

- Find a beautiful gold ribbon and place it in your Bible or some other place where you will see it often. Whenever you notice it, let it gently remind you that with God there is always hope.

Chapter 1

What's Going On?

You are the other part of me
I am the other part of you.
We'll work through
With never a thought of walking out.

RUTH HARMS CALKIN[1]

t was obvious that Erica was uncomfortable. She usually liked curling her feet underneath her while leaning back in a chair and savoring the rich taste of a mocha. But that day Erica sat stiffly with her arms crossed, her beverage ignored, looking sullenly out the window as she thought about my question.

Finally she turned to me with a deep sigh. "Okay, so you want to know what's going on with Jack and me. Well, here it is. Every time I look at him—every time I think about him—I feel sick inside. He's dull and boring and never wants to do anything but go to work, hang out with his friends, or watch television. I have to beg him to do anything around the house, and we constantly fight about the kids. The only time he talks to me is when he wants sex, and then he expects me to be ready the minute he wants to jump in bed."

Erica reached for the familiar comfort of her mocha before continuing. "I don't know how we got this way, but I'm lonely. Oh, God, I am so lonely." And then her voice broke and the tears came.

I (Alice) had known Erica for a long time. We were casual friends, and we occasionally did a few things together as couples. But until she called and asked for help, I had no idea that Erica's marriage was in trouble. We spent most of the rest of that afternoon together discussing the tough questions that were haunting her: "Do you think we ever *really* loved each other? Who is at fault—me or him? What happened to the good times? Even though I feel like walking out, is there any hope for our marriage?"

Facing the Truth

Questions like these are painful and, if you are like most women, you do all you can to avoid asking them. You wanted a wonderful marriage, filled with deep and enduring love. So instead of being completely honest, for a long time you probably tried to ignore the problems, pretending everything was okay. Perhaps you thought, *I just can't deal with that right now, with everything else that's going on.* Perhaps you rationalized that if you minimized your feelings of hurt and disappointment, they would go away.

But the truth is, it is very rare for relationship problems to take care of themselves. Usually the longer you defer acknowledging what is really happening, the more discontentment grows and the more the pain you wanted to avoid deepens. Not tending to marital problems is like not tending to weeds in your garden. When ignored, they can choke out much that is beautiful and good and leave you asking, like Erica, "Is there any hope?"

You probably know that it is important for a husband and wife to talk regularly about the vitality of their marriage and to find out what each one is doing (or not doing) that causes hurt or disappointment to the other. But you may well be at a point that you don't even know how to start such a discussion—or you may feel certain that your partner would never participate. Lack of such communication, in fact, may be part of your pain and frustration in marriage. So we suggest you start somewhere else—with an honest self-evaluation.

As important as it is for a couple to honestly discuss their relationship together, it is equally important for you as a woman to individually look at your own feelings and thoughts. You need to know if you are moving *toward* your husband, *away* from him, or *against* him.

Check Your Symptoms

The checklist on the next page contains twenty thoughts, feelings, and actions that will help you assess whether or not you are in danger of becoming a walk-out woman. We encourage you to answer as honestly as you can, checking the symptoms you have experienced during the last few months. If the symptom occurs frequently, put in two checks.

Keep in mind that some of these symptoms may be caused by circumstances other than your marriage relationship—the death of a family member, moving to a new town, financial reversals, loss of a close friend, career changes, health problems, an empty nest, new goals, or something else. Obviously, if this is true, you should adjust your answers. But be careful of the tendency to rationalize or explain away your unhappiness. If you really think that a symptom is due to your marriage relationship, check it.

Are You in Danger of Walking Away?

Check each symptom that you have routinely experienced over the past few months.

- ❑ Irritation with your husband over trivial matters.

- ❑ Feeling bored, or craving something new and exciting.

- ❑ A strong desire to escape and get away from it all.

- ❑ Loss of energy; feeling tired and worn out.

- ❑ Acting moody and withdrawn around home.

- ❑ Complaining that your husband spends too much time working or watching television.

- ❑ Wanting to begin a career, change jobs, go to school, or move into a new house.

- ❑ Feeling that most conversations with your husband are shallow, angry, or empty.

- ❑ Loss of sexual desire for your husband or feeling that he has lost his desire for you.

- ❑ Desire to change your image (trendy clothes, change in hair color, weight loss, breast augmentation or other cosmetic surgery).

- ❑ Discovering new friends and avoiding old friends with spiritual values.

- ❑ General dissatisfaction with and growing resentment toward your husband.

- ❑ Feeling misunderstood and lonely.

- ❑ Feeling drawn to men who show any form of attention.

- ❑ Imagining what it would be like if you were not married.

- ❑ Tempted by addictive behavior (alcohol, drugs, excess spending, overeating, overexercising, Internet chat rooms, gambling).

- ❑ Sadness about unfulfilled dreams, goals, and expectations.

- ❑ Feeling distant from God and bored or dissatisfied with church.

- ❑ Being nicer, kinder, and more patient to others than to your husband.

- ❑ Spontaneous tearfulness for no apparent reason.

Count the number of boxes you have checked. (If you have double-checked an item, count it only once here, but pay special attention to that item.)

If you checked…   *Your marriage risk is probably…*
1–6   *Mild to moderate—be careful.*
7–12   *Serious—need to make some changes.*
13–20   *Severe—get help now!*

When you've finished the checklist, look at your answers. A few check marks are probably no cause for alarm, although they could be an early warning of problems to be solved. But the more items you checked, the more danger there is for your marriage.

Remember that relationship problems, if left unattended, usually continue to grow. Pain and frustration in your marriage can cause you to close your heart tighter and tighter. Your husband may not know this is happening, and you may not even be completely aware of it.

When couples come to me (Steve) for counseling, I sometimes demonstrate this closing of the heart and emotions by standing up and opening my office door. Then I begin closing the door slowly. Just before it shuts, I pause a moment and then slam it shut completely. The couples jump, but they usually get the message—that it's better to do something before the door slams shut.

The Door Is Still Open

I often ask women who come to me for counseling to read the twenty symptoms and tell me how the list relates to how they feel about their marriage. After one client finished, she had tears spilling out her eyes, running down her cheeks, and dropping off her chin like soft beads. "This is my life," she sobbed. "Every one of your warning signs belongs to me."

As bad as it seemed for the moment, I had good news for her. Because she still cared enough to seek help, it was not too late for her marriage. The same is true for you, whether you checked one or all twenty of the symptoms. The simple fact that you are reading this book tells us that you still care about your marriage, that your heart has not yet slammed shut. We believe that if there is even a tiny flicker of caring—no matter how dim or distant—there is still hope.

You may think it will take a miracle. And that may be true. But we serve a God of miracles. As the prophet Isaiah once wrote, "He has sent Me to…comfort all who mourn…to give them beauty for ashes, the oil of joy for mourning, the garment of praise for the spirit of heaviness."[2]

That is what God can do for your marriage. He can bring beauty out of the ashes of your own pain and disillusionment. But you have to participate in the process.

How do you participate? We are going to ask you to do two simple things for the next three months. Two things only. And for just three months.

First, we'd like you to commit to pray for your husband for fifteen minutes every day.

Second, with the help of a trusted friend or mentor, we'd like you to commit yourself wholeheartedly to work on your marriage by thoroughly digesting this book. In that time, we'd like you to refrain from any discussion or consideration of either divorce or separation.

We are well aware that you might feel reluctant or incapable of managing even these two steps. If so, we ask you to at least read chapter 3, which will help you understand why your husband isn't responding to your needs, and chapter 6, which talks about the heartbreak of divorce. After reading those chapters, you may agree that these are reasonable, even minimal, requests.

If you're worried that you can't pray for *just* your husband for fifteen minutes every day, there are resources available to help you. Some of our favorites are listed in the back of this book. (We strongly recommend Stormie Omartian's book *The Power of a Praying Wife.*) Some women like to use their favorite books on prayer and adapt the prayers for marriage. Another idea is to take your favorite promises from Scripture and rewrite them in your journal as prayers for your marriage. Even the simple process of putting your prayers down on paper can help you focus enough to keep your prayer commitment.

In addition to praying daily, it is vital that you meet at least once a week during the next three months with a trusted friend or mentor who will support you and hold you accountable as you work through this book. Be sure this person is not predisposed to judgment, is full of grace and forgiveness, able and willing to keep your situation confidential, and willing to speak the truth in love. Even though you will probably read this book through more quickly, during your weekly meetings you can use it to focus on solutions that you relate to the most. The section called "Something to Try" at the end of each chapter and the section at the end of the book titled "Coming Alongside" might be helpful for launching conversation.

No matter how busy your schedule, make these times a top priority. If you have young children, you know how distracting they can be, so try to meet while they are in school or make arrangements for someone to watch them for an hour or so.

31

Do I Need to See a Professional?

If you have a great number of the symptoms, if you cannot find a friend you trust, or if you can't even bring yourself at this point to commit three months to your marriage, you may well want to consider seeking perspective from a trained marriage counselor. There are also some specific difficult situations that require immediate help and careful guidance. We call them the "four *As*":

- Abandonment
- Abuse
- Addictions
- Adultery

If you or your husband is struggling with any of these four circumstances, our hearts go out to you. We know there are no easy solutions for these situations, which are not only agonizing, but also complicated. Addictions, for example, are not limited just to drugs and alcohol, but include other obsessions like overspending, gambling, and pornography. With adultery, most people think of a physical affair, but adultery can also mean getting involved at a deep and intimate emotional level. Certainly in our electronic age, Internet affairs can be a real problem. Abandonment is obvious when one of you actually packs his bags, but what about when a spouse is there but *not* there? It is also difficult to define a constant pattern of abuse. You and your children may not be in actual physical danger, but frequent threats or intimidation can put you in a constant state of fear.

We will address the four *A*s again in chapter 7 and talk specifically about affairs in chapter 14. But because these situations are so complex, we believe they call for the help of a trained professional. We encourage you and pray that you will seek such help even if your husband refuses to go with you. Please don't let fear, pride, embarrassment, or worry about finances keep you from it. (Many agencies and offices offer sliding-scale fees to help cover what you cannot afford.)

To find a professional counselor, we suggest you ask for recommendations from your pastor or from other women who have had successful counseling experiences. If you are not satisfied with a particular counselor or are having trouble "connecting" with him or her, don't give up on the process altogether. Try someone else, just as you might do if you didn't have confidence in a medical doctor. At the bottom of this page we have included a list of questions you might use to interview a counselor before your first appointment. Their purpose is to give you a general sense of who the counselor is and whether or not the two of you are a good fit. Feel free to ask your own questions as well. It is important that you feel that the person giving you counsel is trustworthy and confident and embraces the same values that God has placed deep within your heart.[3]

Questions to Ask Your Counselor

- What is your educational background?
- What are your specialty areas?
- How much experience do you have in these areas?
- What is your success rate?
- What is your general approach in working with problems?
- What makes you a good counselor?
- How are you involved in your church?
- How does your faith affect your counseling?
- If married, how would you describe your relationship?

∾ What is your fee schedule?

∾ What kind of payment arrangements are available?

Looking Ahead

Just yesterday, I (Steve) talked to one of my clients who had walked away from her marriage. She and her husband have been back together now for about a month. She said, "I have made some changes, and he has made some changes. Sometimes it seems like we take two steps forward and one step back, but at least we are taking the steps together. We still have a long way to go, but for the first time in more than a year, I'm looking forward to where we are heading."

34

As we write this chapter, we are anticipating what life will be like for you three months from now, and we are excited about the possibilities. Both of us know countless women who have experienced a turnaround in their marriages. And, yes, Erica is among them. Seeing these couples today, you would never believe these women wanted their marriages to end. It is our heartfelt prayer that you will one day know the happiness they are now experiencing.

No matter how you are feeling—even if you are sure love has died—keep reading, keep praying, keep believing. Our God, the miracle maker, still gives beauty for ashes.

Something to Try

You can choose just one...

- Which of the symptoms you checked on pages 26–7 were the hardest for you to admit? What things have you done in the past that improved your symptoms? What makes them worse?

- If your husband is willing, have him look at the symptoms and check the ones *he* thinks you are experiencing. Discuss the differences between his answers and yours. (Note: If your husband is not willing, try to imagine his perspective and see where your answers would differ.)

- If you are willing to make the two-part commitment described on page 30, choose a woman you would look forward to meeting with once a week over the next three months. Call her in the next twenty-four hours. If you are not able to make the two-part commitment at this time, write down a few of the reasons.

- Spend some time browsing in a bookstore, and look through some books on prayer and Scripture promises. (Some ideas are listed in the recommended reading list at the back of this book.) Purchase one that you find inviting and spend some time in it over the next week.

Chapter 2

Lost Dreams

There are two things I've learned:
There is no Cinderella. And, I'm not her Prince.

AUTHOR UNKNOWN

When you were a little girl, did you dream of meeting your Prince Charming, getting married, and living happily ever after? Was being a bride the best part of playing dress-up? Perhaps you fastened a scrap of white lace in your hair, slipped into your mother's high-heeled shoes, and walked down a make-believe aisle scattered with make-believe rose petals.

As a teen, your fantasies about marriage probably changed. You were way past fairy tales at that point. Your ideas were refined while listening to pop songs, watching romantic movies, talking to your friends, and poring over pictures in *Bride's* magazine. And even after you became an adult, your expectations were no doubt shaped by Harlequin romances, daytime soaps, women's magazines, and "chick flicks."

Your personal experiences with marriage, both good and bad, probably shaped your expectations as well. If your parents' marriage was warm and close, you might have expected that for your marriage. If your father was a distant and stoic man or a friendly and talkative one, you might have expected your husband to be the same. If people in your family solved problems with loud debates, a high noise level might seem a normal way to do marriage. If one of your parents let you down in a significant way, you might expect to marry someone who can compensate for that loss.

Whatever your expectations, the marriage you have is probably nothing like what you dreamed it would be. In fact, you may have cut yourself many times on the shards of your own broken dreams and disappointed expectations.

And chances are, your dating experiences probably didn't help. Although dating is meant for getting to know each other, the truth is most people try to show only their best side to their dates. Your husband probably won your heart with affection and tender romance. You won his with admiration and effervescence. He was noble and protective. You were winsome and charming. Conversation sparkled, friendship deepened, pleasure intensified. While still in this romantic haze of young love, it seemed like your marriage would be the dream of a lifetime. Even though you knew that this phase of dizzying love would end, you probably didn't pay much attention to what would come afterward.

What Most Women Want from Their Husbands

The following list is based on our own survey of women from many different backgrounds. How does it compare to your own list of desires?

Respect	Kindness
Provision	Leadership
Communication	Quality time
Sense of humor	Spiritual compatibility
Protection	Integrity
Romance	Affection (sexual and nonsexual)
Friendship	Family involvement

Great (and Not-So-Great) Expectations

It is absolutely normal to have longings and dreams for your marriage. You're *supposed* to have high expectations. Why else would anyone ever want to marry? Even the romantic haze of dating and early love can serve the purpose of bonding you together and building memories to help you through leaner times.

But it's also normal for expectations to be disappointing—because husbands and wives are not perfect, because our expectations are often unrealistic, and also because it's impossible to accurately predict exactly how two people will interact in the intimacy of marriage.

Many marriage experts believe that unrealistic expectations are the number one cause of marital dissatisfaction. Interestingly enough, men usually have a different set of expectations than women do, and it is often the clash of his expectations against hers that makes marriage so difficult. It isn't that the wife is right and the husband is wrong—or the other way around. It's just that most couples have difficulty negotiating the disconnect between expectations and reality.

Disappointed expectations, in other words, are not really the problem. The problem in most marriages is the partners' inability to give up their unrealistic expectations and do what is necessary to help their reasonable expectations become reality.

Les and Leslie Parrott, directors of the Center for Relationship Development at Seattle Pacific University, state, "The belief in a happily-ever-after marriage is one of the most widely held destructive marriage myths. But it is only the tip of the marital-myth iceberg. Every difficult marriage is plagued by misconceptions about what marriage should be."[1] Prior to marriage, the focus is on each other and investing in the relationship. Once you are married, bonding often gets lost in the fray of laundry, dishes, jobs, kids, and other demands of daily living.

For some, the disillusionment comes as early as the wedding night—honeymoon expectations are often disastrous. For others, reality comes like a daily fog, slowly blocking out the sunshine of yesteryear's dreams. Faults overlooked during the whirlwind of dating often loom larger and larger in the routine of everyday life. Personality traits and habits that were once thought attractive can begin to irritate like an itchy rash. Conversation and romance lose their luster. He is tired; you are cranky. He avoids; you push. The simple reality is that maintaining a loving marriage is much harder than falling in love.

> *You'll never see perfection in your mate, nor will he or she find it in you.*
>
> DR. JAMES DOBSON

What You Can Expect

What is reasonable to expect in a marriage, especially a Christian one? We believe it is reasonable for every woman to anticipate that her husband will respect, value, notice, and cherish her, at least most of the time. In fact, God actually instructs husbands to love their wives in such a way that these longings will be fulfilled. In Ephesians, the apostle Paul writes, "Husbands, go all out in your love for your wives, exactly as Christ did for the church—a love marked by giving, not getting."[2]

While God wants a man to support and cherish his wife, a husband cannot be expected to meet *all* her needs or to try to make her happy *all* the time. That is not fair, healthy, or realistic. In fact, it's impossible!

In a warm and wise book celebrating more than fifty years of marriage to Dr. Billy Graham, Ruth Graham writes:

It is a foolish woman who expects her husband to be to her that which only Jesus Christ Himself can be: always ready to forgive, totally understanding, unendingly patient, invariably tender and loving, unfailing in every area, anticipating every need, and making more than adequate provision. Such expectations put a man under an impossible strain. The same goes for the man who expects too much from his wife.[3]

Because your husband is human, it's not realistic to expect him to be perfect. In addition, it's unreasonable and unfair to expect him:

- to read your mind. (He probably can't.)

- to think and feel the same way you do. (He just doesn't.)

- to be just like your father (or anyone else except himself).

- to relate to you the way your girlfriends do. (He's not made that way.)

- to stop responding like a man. (Do you really want him to?)

This last item is important, because a good reality check about how most men function will go a long way to help dispel expectations of a picture-perfect marriage. The fact is that, no matter what, your husband will usually

42

think, act, and talk like a man—and that's a good thing.
Men bring balance to a marriage and usually contribute in
areas such as strength, provision, loyalty, and protection. At
the same time, simply because your husband is a man, you
can probably expect some of these things to be true:

- Because his mind works differently from yours, he
  doesn't naturally understand you, and he may not
  have the faintest idea where to start.

- He may be deeply affected by the wounds of his
  childhood but not comprehend the nature of these
  wounds.

- He may frequently withdraw when you need him the
  most and yet not realize how hurtful, rejecting, or
  confusing this is.

- If you point out a problem or suggest he seek help,
  he may believe you are overreacting, being hyper-
  sensitive, or questioning his masculinity.

- He may not see the seriousness of a relational situation until it becomes a full-blown crisis.

Will every one of these characteristics be true of every
man? Of course not. But these generalities hold true often
enough that they're worth considering—especially because
they are common sources of misunderstanding between
husband and wives. Whether they stem from the way men
are raised in our society or are directly related to the Y

chromosome, they are deeply entrenched. If you can face and understand this reality, you can go a long way toward changing the dynamics of your marriage...and relieving your own disappointed expectations.

Picture Perfect

Award-winning author Grant Howard writes, "We have a picture of the perfect partner, but we marry an imperfect person. Then we have two options. Tear up the picture and accept the person, or tear up the person and accept the picture."[4] If you are considering walking away from the husband you once loved, you might want to ask yourself if you are tearing up the person instead of an unrealistic picture.

Perhaps your disappointment has moved way past irritation over your husband's annoying habits or the loss of romantic love. Maybe your discontentment has gradually deepened over a period of years, and you've begun to regret that you ever married. One woman we spoke to told us she had seriously thought about leaving her marriage nearly every day for more than two years. She was overwhelmed with feeling disappointed, hurt, misunderstood, and unappreciated. Several other women told us they were lonely and angry to the point of despair. They had lost all hope for their marriage and *wanted* to tear up both the person and the picture and start over again. If you are at this point, we urge you to give your marriage more time. For at least three months, sincerely try the two assignments given in the last chapter. In most situations, walking away is a choice that we believe will cause much deeper pain than you are experiencing now.

Another Chance

Denise's first three years of marriage were miserable. One day she grabbed a few of her favorite things, got in the car, and drove away. She had just had one of the biggest arguments of her marriage. She never expected to go back.

Denise spent the night with a close friend from church, who encouraged her to talk to the pastor's wife before making a final decision about walking away from her marriage. During that first meeting, Denise agreed to meet with the pastor's wife once a week for several months.

Twenty years later, Denise says, "Once I decided to let go of my unrealistic dreams and accept Ralph for who he was, I had some tough adjustments to make. He wasn't a knight in shining armor, and our marriage wasn't made in heaven. But I learned to love him—I mean *really love him.* Some of the things that I considered disappointing are now what endear him to me. He is not perfect, yet he has a good heart and is committed to our family. I've learned that these treasures are more valuable than the dreams and expectations I started out with."

If you were to meet Denise and Ralph today, you would never suspect their marriage had such a rocky beginning. If you asked her for advice, Denise would say that you can't expect your husband to be responsible for your happiness, and sometimes you will need to take the initiative for adding excitement and zest to your marriage. I know Denise would want me to encourage you to give your marriage another chance. Remember, your marriage *can* endure through lost dreams, and when it does, it becomes a more treasured kind of love.

Something to Try

You can choose just one...

- Write down what you would consider to be realistic expectations of marriage relationships. Ask someone who has been married for more than thirty-five years to make a list of what she thinks are reasonable expectations. How do your two lists compare?

- Review the sidebar on page 39, "What Women Want from Their Husbands." Add any items that are important to you but don't appear on the list. Then circle the item your husband is very best at. Sometime within the next twenty-four hours, compliment him for this.

- What specific years of your marriage were the very best? What years were the very worst? What years were just average? What do you think are some of the reasons for the difference?

- Ask a friend to do a mug exchange with you. Each of you pick out a pretty coffee mug or teacup, and then exchange them with the pledge that you will pray for each other and for your marriages every time you use them.

Chapter 3

He Doesn't Get It

*While a woman can read
another woman's signals, men can't.
Men aren't even aware that
signals are being sent.*

NANCY COBB AND CONNIE GRIGSBY[1]

What do you do when you've tried everything you know of to communicate your unhappiness to your husband...and he still doesn't seem to get it?

The "clueless male" is an unfortunate stereotype, but like all stereotypes it is based on an element of truth—which is that problems that seem screamingly obvious to you may not be evident to him at all. This is not because he's stupid or because he doesn't care, but because his thought processes are different from yours. He communicates differently than you do—and he listens differently too. This is not only the way God made him, but also the way he's been taught.

If you haven't learned to understand and adjust for these differences, you may well find yourself in a place where you're about ready to walk out while your husband is still in the "we have a pretty good marriage" zone. He may assume that your moodiness is due to PMS, finances, fatigue, stress, or just a stage you are going through—and he may genuinely believe the problems will blow over.

We have seen the following pattern repeated over and over. Because the husband doesn't understand what is bothering his wife so much, he has no clue how to respond to her complaints. When he finally tries to do *something*, it is rarely what the wife really wants. Her hurt deepens, and she closes her heart even more. At the same time, she sends him a message that his efforts are shallow or insincere, that he is doing too little, too late. This makes him feel misunderstood, unappreciated, and confused, and he retreats in frustration—perhaps by working harder and longer at his job, by spending more time with male friends and hobbies, or by just giving up on trying to please his wife.

It's a vicious cycle—but it can be broken. If you have tried and tried and your husband still doesn't seem to "get it," there may be a problem in the way "it" is being communicated.

Buffalo and Butterflies

Part of the reason your husband may seem so clueless is that most men are terrible mind readers, and they aren't much better at picking up on hints. In a man's world, communication is best understood when it is direct, concise, and to the point. Even in business relationships where tact is required, men still get to the bottom line quickly and often boldly. Someone has said that a male's communication is like a buffalo—maybe a little strong, but you sure can't miss it.

When women talk to each other, it's entirely different. They may have their own communication problems, but one of their strengths is intuitively picking up on each other's subtle messages. At the slightest hint of trouble, women notice and begin drawing one another out with nurturing words and thoughtful concern. Signaling a need doesn't have to be bold when you are talking to a woman. It can be as gentle as a butterfly's touch.

With most men, however, those butterfly signals are likely to go unnoticed—again, not because husbands are inherently clueless or have no feelings, but because they are wired differently and have learned to communicate in different ways. It just makes sense, especially when a marriage is headed for trouble, for wives to learn to speak in a language their husbands understand. You need to be bold and, yes, even blunt, but with respect—and without trampling on his heart.

51

If you have an important point to make,
*   don't try to be subtle or clever.*
Use a pile driver. Hit the point once.
*   Then come back and hit it again.*
Then hit it a third time—a tremendous whack.

WINSTON CHURCHILL

Why He Doesn't Hear You

As you are reading this you might be thinking that being too subtle certainly isn't your problem. You have hit the subject hard and hit it again with a tremendous whack. You have spoken clearly and strongly, but he still doesn't get it. That may or may not be true. Perhaps what feels blatant to you is still too indirect for him. Perhaps you have confused directness with whining and nagging, and he has stopped listening as a result. Or possibly something else is going on.

In my twenty-five years of counseling couples, I (Steve) have found there are many reasons why a husband might have trouble hearing truth from his wife. However, the following six are the ones that occur most often.

1. *He may be insecure because of past relationship failures.* The insecurity can date back to when he was a little boy watching his parents handle conflicts. Or his insecurity can be linked to more recent events like a failed romance or previous marriage. He may feel inadequate when it comes to relationships. Avoiding the problem and hoping it will go away may seem better than trying to solve it and failing once again.

2. *He may be reading only one level of communication at a time.* Most women communicate on a number of different levels simultaneously—using words, emotions, and facial expressions, to name just a few. But men tend to listen to only one level at a time. Therefore, when your husband focuses on your words, he may miss the emotions behind the

words. (For instance, he asks if anything is wrong, you *say*, "No, not really"—thinking he can clearly see that something *is* wrong—and he takes you at your word!) Or when he focuses on your emotions, he might be too distracted to catch your words. Sometimes just seeing the expression on your face can block him from hearing what you're saying. Men don't intend to ignore the total message; God just wired them to listen to one level at a time.

3. *He believes that being masculine requires having a solution.* The old joke about men not wanting to ask directions touches on a very basic masculine belief—that they are expected to figure things out on their own. For many men, to ask for help or to indicate that they don't understand something is a statement of personal failure—and to a man in our culture, failure is a terrible thing. It's not just a word describing what he has done; it's a picture of who he is.

4. *He may be in a self-protective mode.* This develops when a wife resorts to intense anger, constant nagging, frequent belittling, or negativity to get what she wants—or when a wife's anger triggers old memories of belittling or negativity. When a husband believes he must defend himself, he often stops listening.

5. *He may be too close to be objective.* Sometimes it takes the input of someone outside the marriage to provide perspective. It is frustrating but true that someone else can say exactly what you have been saying over and over, but your husband won't get it until he hears it from another source.

6. *He may have lost hope.* This is perhaps the saddest reason of all. A husband will stop listening to his wife if he thinks there is nothing he can do to make a difference. Too often we hear men say, "There's nothing I can do to make her happy," or, "I don't know what to do to please her." Instead of trying harder, they just give up.

As you look through these six reasons, perhaps you can identify one or more that apply to your marriage. Once you understand your husband's listening barriers—and perhaps your own failure to communicate clearly—it will be easier to break through them so he can begin hearing your heart.

> Husbands: Pay Attention to...
>   Her words, her wants, her needs, her emotions,
>   her concerns, her preferences, her comfort,
>   her peeves, her friends, her family,
>   her hopes, her dreams.
> Wives: Pay Attention to...
>   His words, his wants, his needs, his emotions,
>   his concerns, his preferences, his comfort,
>   his peeves, his friends, his family,
>   his hopes, his dreams.

Helping Him Hear You

We wish that getting your husband to really hear you could be as easy as handing him his half of the sidebar listed above. But, of course, it isn't that easy. Communicating your frustrations with your husband will require patience, skill, and determination on your part. It may require that you learn some new methods of talking and listening. If you can accomplish this, the rewards for your marriage can be immense.

Before you start, try to accept the fact that your husband's method of hearing and listening is not necessarily wrong; it's just different. In your mind, grant him the right to be different. Instead of branding him as "clueless," resolve to speak to him in a way he can hear.

It also helps to plan what you want to say. Because men typically respond to bottom-line communication and tend to be problem solvers, we suggest you spend some time focusing on your own relational bottom line. Ask yourself specifically what you need most from your husband at this particular time. Depending on how you process things, you may want to do this all at one sitting or brainstorm for a couple days. Write down everything that comes to mind in random order. Next, organize the list by grouping similar items together. Finally, choose the most important ones and succinctly state them on a separate sheet of paper. This will be your cheat sheet for communicating your needs in a way that your husband can hear.

Once you have honed your list, here are some essential steps to effectively communicating the items on it.

Choose a time and place. I (Alice) always found that Saturday mornings were a good time to have serious discussions with Al. When our kids were still at home, we made arrangements for them to be at someone else's house for a couple hours. I chose mornings because it gave us a whole day to process rather than tackling heavy conversation right before bedtime. Having breakfast and lingering for a bit over coffee set a mood of camaraderie instead of combativeness.

That's what worked for us, but your situation may be different. Just try to choose a time and place where you are both refreshed, have privacy, and are not rushed.

Give him a chance. Many times we become so self-absorbed with our own problems that we forget that others are hurting too. You might start the conversation by saying you are concerned about your marriage and you want to know if he has any suggestions for what would make it better. In other words, you want to know what he needs from you. Give him the choice of telling you right then or thinking about it for forty-eight hours and then getting back to you. If he answers right away, listen completely without protest or defense. (You want to model good listening skills, sincerity, and concern.) Have a pencil and paper handy, and tell him you are going to write down the key points so you won't forget them.

Calmly and clearly communicate your needs. Try to remain calm so your husband is not distracted by your emotions and misses the content. (If you are very upset and emotional, it might be a good idea to talk this whole thing out with a friend first.) And make your point as clearly and concisely as you can. Someone once said, "Women often verbalize a series of items in random order, listing all the options and possibilities at the same time." Men tend to be overwhelmed by the sheer volume of such information and stop listening. You'll get a better response if you discipline yourself to focus on four things:

- What you need
- How you need it
- When you need it
- Why you need it

When you are addressing painful or emotional issues, it might be a good idea to monitor your tone of voice when you speak. Because women have higher voices in the first place and because tension can tighten the voice, it's easier for you to resort to whining or screeching tones that are hard for anyone to listen to. Focus on keeping your voice low and gentle, and you'll have a better response.

Ask for feedback. Sometimes the best part of a discussion follows questions like: "Well, what do you think? Am I being fair? Unfair? Do you think I'm being ridiculous?" Then, ask your husband what he heard you say. This would be a great time to use the same list above to ask him his needs. But don't press him to answer right away if he's not ready. Men do not typically process things verbally the way women do, and they often feel the need to think before responding to a situation. It's better to set a time for him to get back to you than to press for answers right now. Remember to model the listening skills you would like him to use with you.

Reach his long-term memory. Your husband probably stores problems in his short-term memory because he likes things that can be fixed quickly. He tends to think that if he does what you want a few times, then everything is okay. You need to reach his long-term memory by stating specifically that this is not just how you are feeling today or how you are feeling because of what he did or didn't do yesterday. He needs to know that these are concerns you have had for a long time. If you have been struggling with negative feelings for six months, tell him. If it's been a year or more, tell him.

Express your fears. Don't threaten him or lay down an ultimatum—because men usually respond to threats with anger or stubbornness. But tell him specifically that if these problems aren't resolved, you are concerned that they will get worse. Tell him that you are afraid you will grow apart from each other and love will be lost.

Paint a word picture if you can. This technique has been used to great advantage by some women. Instead of nagging or repeating yourself, try a more vivid approach to describe how you feel. For instance, tell him you feel like you are lost in the woods. You are alone and it's growing dark and every path you have tried only leads you further away. You are afraid and you need him to help you find the way back home.

Plan to meet again in forty-eight hours. Ask your husband if he will think and pray about what you have said and plan a second meeting in no more than forty-eight hours to discuss a game plan. At the second meeting, you will find out if he is willing to change and make something happen. If he is, decide how you can work together toward a goal. Be very specific about what, how, and when. Write out your plan. Help him do his part by using encouragement and positive reinforcement rather than criticism and nagging.

If He Still Doesn't Get It

Change takes time, and breaking ineffective communication patterns will not happen overnight. You might need to repeat the steps listed above several times before your husband really begins to hear you. But if there is only minimal response over the next few weeks, if your husband consistently breaks his promises to get back to you, or if he resists talking to you at all, you may need the help of a third person to get your husband to understand the seriousness of the situation.

Your church may be able to recommend a mature couple to meet with you and your husband for a number of months, or your pastor may be able to provide guidance. If this does not succeed, it is probably time to consider seeking the help of a trained counselor. If your husband will not go with you, go alone. A trained individual will be able to give you valuable advice for your specific situation.

We understand that sometimes you won't feel like trying to get through to your husband because you're too discouraged and you just want to give up. Although our hearts ache with you, we urge you to hang in there a little longer. You might be wonderfully surprised at how your husband responds once he finally hears you.

Something to Try

You can choose just one...

- List the signs that tell you your husband is truly listening to you. Then list the signs that tell you he isn't listening. Cook him a favorite meal or take him to his favorite restaurant. After you have eaten, respectfully share your lists with him.

- The next time your husband is in the mood to talk, practice listening for five-minute segments with no interruptions except to ask him noncombative questions. During these times, listen to:

  - His words
  - His comfort level
  - His emotions
  - His tone of voice
  - His concerns
  - His dreams

- On pages 52–54, review the six common reasons why a man might have trouble hearing truth from his wife. Which ones do you think might apply to your husband?

- One woman said that when she got married, her mother's advice was, "Don't forget your girlfriends." Why don't you round up a couple of friends early Saturday morning and hit the local yard sales and flea markets. It's fun and inexpensive. Who knows what treasures you will find—in addition to the much-needed camaraderie?

Chapter 4

What Happened to the Good Times?

*It's never too late—
in fiction or life—
to revise.*

NANCY THAYER

her name could be Sandy or Melanie or Glenna. She could be married for less than a year, about six years, or as many years as it took to reach the time when her youngest child is preparing for college. She isn't crying, but there were probably many nights of crying before she reached this point.

"I'm just not in love anymore," she says. "It's not that I want to hurt him, but I don't think I can go on like this. We hardly ever speak to each other, and when we try, there doesn't seem to be anything to talk about. Sometimes I wonder if we ever really loved each other."

Before and after Marriage

When my friends and I (Alice) talk about how we met our husbands, we all have stories about "tracking them down." In my case, Al was a nearby neighbor, and I could see his backyard from my kitchen window. If I noticed he was outside working, I would run a comb through my hair, apply fresh lipstick, and clip the leash on Sloopy, my miniature collie. As soon as we reached the edge of Al's property, I would unclip the leash, hoping Sloopy would run into his backyard. It never worked. Sloopy ran everywhere but there.

Al was a nice guy. He had always been nice. Eventually we met (on a day when I looked a mess and Sloopy was nowhere in sight), became best friends, and married. Around the time of our first anniversary, I was having coffee with my friend Maggie. We had known each other since before kindergarten, and whenever we got together our jaws would fly at eighty-five miles an hour. On this particular day I happened to be mad at Al, so I started ragging about everything negative in our marriage…and about him. If Maggie had asked me to name one good thing about Al that day, my mind would have gone blank.

After about twenty minutes of listening to my tirade, Maggie said something that I still remember more than thirty-five years later. "You thought Al was so great before you were married. What has happened to him since he married you?"

Her question stopped me cold. *What happened?* With

gentle words, Maggie started coaxing me to think about more positive memories, starting back when I had tried so hard to get Al to notice me. It was amazing how remembering those fun times softened my heart. To this day, I'm grateful to my dear friend, who helped me focus on the positive parts of our marriage.

> Married life...is a mosaic of little things.
> Little touches.
> Little words.
> Little smiles of encouragement.
> Little expressions of endearment.
>
> NANETTE KINKADE[1]

63

Souvenirs of the Heart

One of the reasons marriages get into trouble—why there is a *falling out of love*—is because our thoughts get stuck on what is wrong instead of what is right. Jesus said, "The mouth speaks out of that which fills the heart,"[2] and this is certainly true in marriage. If we keep rehearsing our hurts and dwelling on negative thoughts, we soon follow up with hurtful words—and the damaging echoes of those words continue for a long time. This negative-type momentum can happen anytime, but there are five stages when a marriage is particularly vulnerable.

1. *Before your first anniversary.* Many women find that the first year of marriage is the hardest. He has his ways; she

has hers. It takes time to learn together and develop new ways that belong to them both. When faced with the reality of living with her husband's imperfections and bad habits, a new bride may begin to think she has made a terrible mistake. She may be tempted to get out before becoming more invested.

2. *First year of firstborn.* Nurturing and caring for a newborn can be exhausting. To some new moms, it can also seem more satisfying than the marriage relationship. On top of this, the husband may want more attention and/or sex than the wife is willing or able to give. Routines are disrupted, and he feels left out. When he sulks, she detaches herself emotionally. Soon they both are caught up in a cycle of expecting too much and getting too little.

3. *The "seven-year itch."* It doesn't always happen at seven years—but it usually happens somewhere between the fifth and ninth year. This is the point when marriage typically becomes routine and falls into a rut and both individuals feel like they are being taken for granted. Romance may flicker like a candle about to burn out, and boredom and restlessness may set in. Either partner may begin to ask, "Is this all there is?"

4. *Launching the youngest child.* Getting ready to launch the youngest child, or the first year of an empty nest, can be one of the most stressful times in a woman's life. This is especially true when she has defined her identity mostly through the role of motherhood. During this period of adjustment, she often feels lonely and starts searching for

something to make her existence meaningful again. As she evaluates who she is, what she enjoys doing, and what her dreams are, she may get caught up in plans that she thinks would work better if she were not married or were married to someone else.

5. *Extended periods of stress.* It can stem from financial reverses, the heartbreak of prodigal children, caring for elderly parents, health problems, or long periods of having too much to do. The wife sometimes becomes so weary that she is unable to think or care about what is good about her marriage. Her memory of the good times grows dim, the distance grows, and a worn-out woman is at risk of becoming a walk-out woman.

65

Asking Questions

- What attracted you and your husband to each other?

- What made you fall in love?

- How did the two of you behave when your relationship was strong?

- What were some of the most terrific moments of your relationship?

- How would you treat your best friend if you started having problems?

DR. LINDA S. MINTLE[3]

During times like these, it is easy to rewrite the history of your marriage. Memories of endearing moments and happy times are replaced with memories of ugly arguments and unending disappointments. If you are feeling out of love, could it be that you have sorted through the souvenirs of your heart and thrown away the treasures?

Falling in Love Again

For many of you, the road to falling out of love has been long and you don't feel like trying to love again. For others, it isn't a matter of rewriting the history of your marriage—the truth is that the sad memories outweigh the happy ones. You simply don't feel like any effort on your part is worth the cost. In both of these situations, love can still grow and thrive. The wonderful thing about starting to fall in love again is you don't have to *feel* love at the beginning. Instead, you *do* love. *Doing* love doesn't change the past, but it often changes the future.

Can you choose to do some positive things for your husband and your marriage? Can you try for a few months and see what happens? Here are some simple ways to remind yourself of happy times and jump-start a more positive attitude.

Ask yourself some questions. At one time, you and your husband probably were friends. Just remembering that fact is a good starting point. Next, ask the questions in the sidebar on page 65. At first, just ask them of yourself, and then, when you are ready, discuss your answers with your husband.

Notice his good points. I (Steve) frequently use a list of a hundred positive attributes in my counseling practice. This list contains words like *active, adaptable, adventurous, ambitious, attractive*—right through the alphabet to *well-read, wise, witty, zestful.* Make a point of looking for such positive attributes in your husband. If you keep a journal, we suggest setting aside a page or two just to list your husband's good points when they occur to you. When you are offering praise in your daily prayers, thank God that your husband has these good characteristics. And don't forget to mention the positive traits you notice to your husband too.

Reminisce. If you have a collection of photographs or do scrapbooking, spend some leisurely hours looking through them and remembering the good times—really think about them. What was the occasion, what did you wear, what was the weather like? Especially notice the pictures where you and your husband were snuggled together or holding hands. Let your heart feel the warmth of those special moments. Consciously remember what you were to one another.

Make some new memories. If your husband is willing, plan a small date. Just the two of you—a slow walk in the moonlight or going out to a favorite place for a hot-fudge sundae. Keep the conversation light. Look kindly at his face and remind yourself that this is the face you once loved. Touch his cheek. Trace his eyebrows with your finger. Hold hands.

All of the above ideas are little beginnings, like taking the first steps on a new path that you hope will lead someplace wonderful. Later there is a whole chapter that has more in-depth suggestions for "reconnecting." For now, the important thing to realize is that there were good times in the past and there can be even better times in the future.

Phillip McGraw, host of the popular television show *Dr. Phil,* writes, "Claim the courage to be the one who reaches across the table and takes your partner's hand and says, 'I want to talk about falling in love with you all over again.'"[4]

Who knows, these may be the most important words that you will ever say to your husband.

Something to Try

You can choose just one...

∽ Remember the circumstances when you and your husband first met. What attracted you to him? The next time you are with friends, ask how they met their husbands and then have fun telling how you met yours.

∽ Think about the concept behind the list of a hundred positive attributes mentioned on page 67. Write out at least five things that you respect about your husband, and look for ways to share them with him during the next few days.

∽ Take the time to look through some of your photographs or scrapbooks. Choose one of the best times you and your husband have ever shared, and answer these questions:

- When was it?

- Where were you?

- What made it so great?

∽ Select a favorite photograph of you and your husband. Go to a secondhand store or craft shop, and find a unique frame for the picture. Put it someplace where you will see it often, and use it as a reminder that you can fall in love with him all over again.

Chapter 5

Keeping Score

When you're in love, you put up with things that,
when you're out of love you cite.

JUDITH MARTIN (MISS MANNERS)

ast night Tami and I (Steve) watched a rerun of one of our favorite shows, *Everybody Loves Raymond.* This episode featured the wedding of Raymond's brother. The marriage celebration became one gigantic fiasco—not just funny bloopers, but sarcastic, hurtful stuff, all captured on the wedding video. But later, as Raymond toasted the bride and groom, he gave some good advice that applies to every relationship. He said something like, "Marriage is full of a lot of stuff that you really don't want to remember. So just keep the good parts and edit out the bad. Please don't save the bad pictures—just the good ones."

Editing out the bad pictures isn't so easy. Women are more likely to look at them again and again—evaluating and sorting them in stacks of good and bad, positive and negative—constantly checking to see which stack is higher. This process isn't necessarily deliberate, or even conscious; it's just part of a natural feminine tendency to keep close tabs on the status of relationships. Even everyday habits like a man's manners and cleanliness are subconsciously evaluated and can cause a woman to draw closer or pull away from her husband.

In his classic book *His Needs, Her Needs,* author Willard Harley Jr. refers to this evaluation process as a love bank. Harley writes, "Each person either makes deposits or withdrawals whenever we interact with him or her. Pleasurable interactions cause deposits, and painful interactions cause withdrawals."[1]

Love Bank Conversations

- What gifts could we give each other that would be most meaningful?

- What could we do for each other that would be most appreciated?

- Where would you like to go on a dream vacation?

- What could we do to make our relationship more romantic?

- How can I help your dreams come true?[2]

When you are in an affectionate and caring relationship, regular deposits are made in your love bank. The balance is positive, and you think your marriage is good. The higher the balance, in fact, the better you feel. This is how love grows. If, on the other hand, you feel ignored or mistreated or sense that your basic needs are not met, withdrawals are made. If withdrawals exceed deposits, the balance in your love bank becomes negative and you feel angry, hurt, or disconnected. You may think you're a fool for staying in the relationship, or you may decide that staying is okay as long as you remain emotionally distant. Either way, if a negative balance lasts too long, your heart closes, and love begins to die.

Everybody has a love bank—but as we have seen, wives tend to keep closer tabs on the balances. In our experience, husbands seldom know the balance of their wives' love banks—or their own, for that matter. If they are aware of it at all, they tend to overestimate their deposits in their wives' accounts and to underestimate their withdrawals. That is what was happening with Jolene and Eddie, a couple who recently came to me (Steve) for counseling.

73

Making the Grade

It wasn't Eddie's idea to come to my office. When Jolene first suggested counseling to him, Eddie said no because he thought she was the one with problems. When I called and explained that talking to both of them together would be better for finding solutions, he finally agreed to come. He sat across from me with jaws clenched—his expression clearly showing what he was thinking: *I've tried and there is absolutely no way to please this woman.*

Jolene glared at him through angry tears and said

accusingly, "You don't even know what it means to take me on a real date. Sure, we went to a nice restaurant and you spent a lot of money, but you didn't talk to me. You didn't comment about how I looked or hold my hand even for a minute. As far as I'm concerned, the whole evening was a waste of time and money."

What Eddie didn't realize was that he had scored a big minus when it came to meeting his wife's needs. In his mind, their evening out was just that—an evening out. But while he was savoring the taste of his prime rib, Jolene was tasting nothing but disappointment. Once again it seemed to her that Eddie wasn't interested in her or her needs and concerns.

Jolene's criteria for evaluating the evening grew out of her desire for meaningful conversations and nonsexual romance. Because Eddie frequently ignored these issues, Jolene felt he didn't really care about her. As a result, he was making regular withdrawals from her love bank, and as the balance dropped, Jolene was pulling away. She managed to be preoccupied when Eddie was around, lost interest in their hobbies, and resented the time he spent with his friends. Eddie was perplexed by these changes, but he never connected them to his behavior. He just considered them part of the mysterious and unexplainable moodiness of women. He didn't know how to find out what she really needed from him and so fell short of the mark whenever he tried to please her. After that last dinner date, he was so confused that he just gave up, hoping she would snap out of *her* problems.

In fairness to Eddie, Jolene's "accounting" system had taken on some dangerous characteristics. Although it is common for women to subconsciously keep score, the tendency toward negative history keeping can make difficult situations seem even worse.

What do we mean by negative history keeping? It's simply the tendency to look back and focus exclusively on the hurts and disappointments in your marriage. The more challenging a marriage becomes, the easier it becomes to see only the love withdrawals and not even notice the deposits. A few bad actions can get projected into an infinite pattern of bad behaviors. All the good that your husband does becomes eclipsed by his failures.

When you magnify your husband's faults and minimize his strengths, you lose perspective. You may even come to believe that your husband doesn't love you, when he loves you very much—and your chronic unhappiness will irritate you as well. As King Solomon said, "If you search for good, you will find favor; but if you search for evil, it will find you!"[3]

Relationships are full of all kinds of memories—some good, some bad, some neutral. Yet looking back on your history through a negative lens is like looking through a dirty window: Everything appears darker and dingier than it actually is. This sort of dark accounting closes your mind to the possibility of improvement, and the future of your relationship appears to be a hopeless continuation of the past.

*We all desire to be remembered
for our best moments.*

AUTHOR UNKNOWN

Grading with Grace

Every marriage stumbles from time to time. One of the biggest challenges during these times is that strict accounting comes naturally, and grace doesn't. Grace involves giving gifts of mercy and patience when these are the last things you want to give. It sometimes means judging your husband less harshly than he deserves and doing your best to look past the dark-colored memories that trouble you.

When I (Steve) was in college, I took several classes from a professor who was highly respected not only for his knowledge, but also for his kindness and consideration. At the beginning of the semester he always announced, "Everyone in this class starts off with an A. Your job is to maintain it. There will be weekly exams, but at the end of the quarter, I'll erase your two lowest grades."

This professor wasn't a pushover. Far from it. His grace-filled approach usually got wonderful results from his students. We did everything we could to please him. I have seen this happen in countless marriages as well. When partners operate on a system of grace rather than keeping strict accounts, their happiness often increases dramatically.

What does that mean in practical terms? Here are some ideas:

Give your husband (and yourself) a fresh start.
Consciously erase his negative balance in your love bank—
in fact, give him some extra points. Try to believe the best
about him. Assume that he wants to be a good husband to
you. (He probably does.) While you're at it, give yourself a
positive balance too.

Does this mean you will instantly be able to forget the
hurts of the past? Of course not. But we've found that adopt-
ing this "positive balance" attitude as a starting point can
really make a difference in how you view your relationship.

*Do your best to communicate your reasonable needs
clearly.* Explain why they are so important to you and what
your husband can do to meet them. See chapters 2 and 11
for more ideas on how to do this.

Be sure you give your husband credit for deposits he has made
and even for his good intentions. Celebrate what he does
well. Don't let negative history keeping blind you to your
husband's good points.

Do your best to erase some of his bad performances. We are
not suggesting denial. The memories will still be there. But
you can choose not to be obsessed with them, to simply let
them go. For more on the subject of releasing past hurts,
see chapter 7.

At the same time, obviously, your husband has some
work to do. He needs to pay more attention to how his
behavior affects you. He must learn to understand your
needs. And of course, he needs to extend grace to you as well.

Remembering that men are usually not good at asking

directions, you probably need to coach him a little. The following questions may not be the sort your husband will think of on his own. We suggest sharing the following list with him at a neutral time and telling him they are some of the best questions he can ask you on a regular basis:

- How is our marriage?

- What do you need today?

- How can I be a better husband?

As your husband learns how to make more deposits and you learn to do your accounting with grace, you will be amazed at how quickly your love bank starts filling up again. Soon you will notice that it is easier to follow the advice Raymond gave his brother—to keep the good parts and edit out the bad.

"Please don't save the bad pictures—just the good ones."

After all, that's what grace is all about.

Something to Try

You can choose just one...

- What are some of the bad pictures in your marriage that you need to edit out? What are some of the good pictures you need to focus on and celebrate?

- What have you done lately to make deposits in your husband's love bank? List three things *he* would consider deposits.

  _____

  _____

  _____

- What have you done lately that has made withdrawals from your husband's love bank? List three things *he* would consider withdrawals.

  _____

  _____

  _____

- Make or buy your husband's favorite dessert, and find a time when the two of you won't be interrupted. While you are sitting together and enjoying the dessert, ask each other the questions in the "love bank conversations" sidebar on page 72.

Chapter 6

The Downside of Divorce

*To love and to cherish...forsaking all others...
in sickness and in health...for richer, for poorer...
for better or worse...so long as you both shall live.*

Traditional marriage vows

Carla reached into her purse and pulled out a small framed picture taken twelve years before. At age fourteen Carla had been taller than her mother and extremely attractive. In the picture, she had a big grin on her face. Her two younger brothers, her mom and dad, and Carla were bundled up in hats and gloves, snuggling close together on a snow-covered porch with Christmas lights wound around the wooden railing.

That photo was taken the last Christmas her whole family had been together. Carla remembered that she had always loved living in that house. After her parents divorced, however, she and her brothers had moved five times before she graduated from high school.

Even with the numerous moves, Carla did well in school. She finished college and now enjoys a satisfying career. She lives in a nice condominium and is proud of the secondhand furniture that she refinished herself, but she's more or less put her personal life on hold after a series of painful breakups.

Carla's mom remarried shortly after the divorce, but that relationship lasted less than two years. Her older brother still lives at home and helps with yard work and small repairs around the house. Since dropping out of high school, he's drifted from job to job, always with a promise of going back to school sometime soon. Her younger brother lives with his girlfriend in her parents' home. They are helping Carla's brother and their daughter out until they can save enough money to get married and raise their six-month old baby on their own.

Carla slowly ran her finger around the picture frame and then looked up, commenting that just yesterday her mom had said, "Sometimes I wonder how things would have turned out if your dad and I had stayed married."

With a catch in her voice Carla said, "I wonder that too."

Eight Resolutions for Your Marriage

1. Never purposely hurt each other.

2. Let go of past hurts.

3. Apologize when needed.

4. Initiate fun, excitement, and surprises.

5. Support each other in public.

6. Praise each other to family and friends.

7. Look your best for each other.

8. Never use the word *divorce.*

Revealing Research

In their provocative book *The Case for Marriage,* Linda J. Waite and Maggie Gallagher gathered strong scientific research supporting the fact that even in "high conflict" marriages—excluding those involving abuse—divorce generally creates more problems than it solves. A key piece of this research indicates that high-conflict marriages usually improve if the couples stick it out. In fact, 86 percent of unhappily married people reported that after five years their marriages became much happier. This was true even for those who rated their marriages "very unhappy." Five years later, 77 percent of these people had changed their rating to "very happy" or "quite happy."[1]

Linda Waite, a sociology professor at the University of Chicago, sums up these findings by saying, "Just because you're not getting along now doesn't mean that if you get divorced things will get better. And, it doesn't mean if you stay together things will stay this bad. The chances that they'll get worse are low, and the chances that they'll get better are almost overwhelming."[2]

That research is good news. God's ideal for marriage has always been one man, one woman, for a lifetime.

How About You?

If you are at the point where your heart is already closed toward your husband, you will probably find this a difficult chapter to accept. You might wrestle with thoughts like: *God wants me to be happier than this. Once we get through the divorce, the children will adjust. In the long run, everyone will be better off.* But the honest truth is that divorce is a tragedy with painful repercussions for everyone involved. More important, its advantages rarely outweigh its negative impact.

Divorce is ugly even when it's between two nice people. The notion of a "good divorce" is a definite oxymoron. Whether it is the man who walks away or the woman who leaves, the very nature of divorce places a couple in an antagonistic position and forces each of them to look after his or her own personal (and, yes, frequently selfish) interests. Obviously these actions are in direct contradiction to their marriage vows of honoring and caring for one another through all the joys and heartaches of life.

Before moving on to the rest of this chapter, please take a moment to carefully read the small list beginning on page 82 called "Eight Resolutions for Your Marriage."[3] Every item on this list is essential for keeping your marriage healthy and alive. However, at this point we are asking you to focus on the last five words: "Never use the word *divorce.*"

This is a promise that Tami and I (Steve) made to each other years ago. It was also a promise we made to our children as we sat at the kitchen table one Saturday morning. The day before, our daughter Brittany and a friend had been talking about how hard it would be if their parents got a divorce and they had to choose between living with their mom or dad. When we heard about that, we gathered our children together and promised them that no matter what, we would never use the word *divorce* in our marriage.

I want to encourage you to go one step further than I did on that Saturday morning. Never allow yourself to even *consider* the word *divorce*.

The Deadly Fallout of Divorce

There are many reasons why we believe divorce is a choice you will regret. Following are six that occur most often in our research.

1. *Divorce devastates your children.* Although it is common to assume that children are resilient and "bounce back" after divorce, many recent studies reveal that divorce leaves children with lifelong scars. The reality is that kids (regardless of their ages) are innocent victims of divorce, and yet they often blame themselves for the failure of their parents' marriage. At the same time, they lose the constant presence of one parent. They may also lose their home, their church, their standard of living, their sense that life is secure, and their role models for lasting love and healthy relationships. As a result, children of divorce have a higher probability of being abused, having difficulty in school,

struggling with depression, acting out violently, getting involved in promiscuity, falling into addictions, failing in their marriages, and rejecting their parents' faith.[4]

2. *Divorce confuses and disconnects other people too.* Family members and friends feel like they have to choose sides, and they feel disloyal if they still love and respect the left-behind spouse. "My heart is broken," said the mother of a walk-out woman. "I love her so much, but she will never understand how hard this is for me." Many times the extraordinarily valuable interaction between grandparents and grandchildren is compromised or ruined.

3. *Divorce is a financial disaster*—especially for women. It's obvious that it costs more for a couple or family to live apart than to live together. Sometimes the family home has to be sold and other assets divided. Add in the lawyers' fees, and from a purely monetary position, divorce doesn't make sense. The impact on everyone's self-esteem and the adjustment in quality of life is far more severe than most women ever think possible. Because women usually retain custody of children and because women usually earn less than men, the majority of divorced women experience a dramatic drop in their standard of living—as much as 27 percent, while men typically gain about 10 percent.[5]

One person summed it up this way: When you think of the thousands of dollars a couple spends on divorce proceedings, how much better if that money were spent on marriage counseling and attempts at reconciliation. Another says, "Divorce is much more financially devastating than most wives can ever imagine. I know because I've been there."

4. *Divorce rarely solves the problem.* It's tempting to believe that divorce is easier than keeping the marriage together, but that's simply not true. Running away rarely solves problems; we carry them with us like heavy suitcases. If you had communication problems in your marriage, chances are you will continue to have communication problems. If there are intimacy issues in marriage, those issues are likely to follow you out of the marriage.

No matter how painful your relationship has become, you really do have a choice. You can stay in the marriage and work on the issues where you are. Or you can leave and work on those same issues in a different situation—with all the added pain and devastation created by the divorce itself.

> The real winners in life are the people
> who look at every situation
> with an expectation that they can
> make it work or make it better.
>
> BARBARA PLETCHER[6]

5. *Divorce sets you up to repeat your difficulty.* It may be tempting, while in the throes of a painful marriage, to assume that things would be better with someone else. But research shows just the opposite. The truth is that second marriages have about a 60 percent failure rate.[7] And that percentage increases exponentially for third or fourth marriages. Too often the complaints heard about a first

marriage are the same complaints that develop in subsequent relationships.

6. *Divorce often weakens your faith.* Knowing that God hates divorce[8] (especially when there are no biblical grounds), it is not uncommon for a walk-out woman to distance herself from church and Christian friends. As her pride and self-esteem tumble, she may become like a lonely ember separated from the fire, and her faith may slowly turn cold.

The school of life, as well as many passages in the Bible, teaches us that difficulties help us grow. But walking away from our problems usually does just the opposite. It promotes immaturity because we escape the challenges and hard work of perseverance and patience. Yes, it is natural to look for a way out when facing adversity, but choosing to remain steadfast builds character and helps us discover the great faithfulness of God. God has set eternity in our hearts,[9] and He is preparing us for *there* instead of providing us with what we call happiness *here*. Unfortunately the choice between happiness and godliness is not always easy.

We realize that some of you reading this chapter are in such dire circumstances that you must leave. If that's true—if you've carefully and prayerfully considered your options, sought counseling, done everything you can to make your marriage work—then we certainly aren't sitting in judgment. The road before you will be hard, and we hope you will rely on your heavenly Father, who loves you no matter what, to comfort you and guide you and help you grow through this new kind of adversity.

But before you reach that point, we pray that you will think very hard about the consequences of divorce. We have found that people who think about walking away usually minimize the consequences of divorce. They believe they can beat the odds and make another marriage work or that their children will get through the trauma of divorce without any scars. They rationalize away their moral and religious beliefs by saying that God wants them to be happy, and yet they make a choice that leaves a wide path of pain for others.

You may think it would take a miracle to fix your marriage. But again, God is in the miracle business and nothing is impossible with Him. With His help, you can not only survive, but actually thrive in your marriage.

The Bible says that we leave an inheritance to our children's children.[10] If you intentionally leave your marriage and forsake the vows you made on your wedding day, you leave an inheritance of regret. We don't know anyone who is proud of his or her divorce.

But if you stay in your marriage and with God's help it turns around, think of the wonderful inheritance you will leave for others—a legacy of faith and faithfulness. That is truly a rich and worthy gift to pass along to future generations.

Something to Try

You can choose just one...

- Write down as many lines from your wedding vows as you can remember. Then choose one of the following statements that best describes how you consider your marriage vows:

  - A covenant with God

  - A commitment to each other

  - A marriage tradition

  - A romantic fantasy

- This chapter lists six reasons, based on research, why divorce may be cause for regret. Are there some that concern you more than others?

- Which of the "resolutions for your marriage" listed on pages 82–3 are the easiest for you to keep? Which are the hardest?

- Before you fall asleep tonight, take time to list four or five things that you were grateful for during the day. Or, if you keep a gratitude journal on a regular basis, scan over some of your past entries to give yourself a cheerful lift.

Chapter 7

It Hurts So Much

God cushions our hurting hearts
with soft pillows of comfort and hope.

JUDY GORDON[1]

O ne of the hit movies in 2003 was *Bruce Almighty,* starring Jim Carrey. In the story, Jim's character takes his girlfriend (played by Jennifer Aniston) for granted, ignores her feelings, and hurts her deeply. In a moving scene, Jennifer prays that God will take her love away. She begs God to help her stop loving Jim because loving him just hurts too much.

Love isn't easy. Sometimes you find that the more you care, the more you hurt. In fact, relationships can be so full of disappointments that you feel discouraged most of the time. You might even start wishing that you had never met your husband, had never fallen in love, and certainly had never married. When tears and heartaches fill your hours, you too might find yourself wishing you could just stop loving this man who hurts you so.

Powerful Emotions

Emotions in themselves aren't good or bad. They just are. Our feelings let us know that we are alive and that our hearts are touched by what happens around us. But negative emotions can also overwhelm us, especially when our marriages are troubled. One reason for this is the closeness of the relationship. The time you spend together, the intimacies you share, and what you have invested in the relationship make you more vulnerable to emotional highs and lows. Depending on your husband's actions or attitudes, you can feel wonderful peace or excruciating pain all within a few hours—or even a few moments.

It's important to realize that every marriage has hurts, but when they are left unattended, they accumulate and escalate, fueling both anger and depression. They can develop into an anxious obsession, smothering love and leading you to believe that the only way to survive is to walk away from the person who is causing you pain.

Although King David's words aren't about marriage, his emotions might sound familiar to you. When things got rough, even a king thought about walking away:

> My heart is in anguish…
> "Oh, that I had the wings of a dove!
> I would fly away and be at rest—
> I would flee far away…
> far from the tempest and storm."[2]

In many ways, difficult emotions can be more painful than a physical injury. Our friend Keely writes, "When you are hurting, your heart feels as though it will break into a thousand pieces—or just stop working altogether." Some of the clients I (Steve) see in my practice say there are times when they feel so much pain they wonder if they are going crazy or if they might even die. No wonder their first thought is to escape in some way—in any way. Emotions can be so intense that they distort your thinking and tempt you to consider options that are irrational, unhealthy, or in direct opposition to your core values.

> Like anyone else, I have days when discouragement seems
> to get the better of me.
> At such times I try to remember that the Lord has provided
> me with a source of continuing inspiration and hope.
> To tap into that source I need simply to open the pages
> of my Bible, God's letter of hope to me.
>
> SHIRLEY DOBSON[3]

A hundred different acts and attitudes can trigger hurt in a marriage. The women we interviewed for this book mentioned insensitivity, forgetfulness, neglect, meanness, disrespect, betrayal, and more. Every situation was unique, and it was interesting to discover that what profoundly wounded one person hardly bothered someone else. However, every woman who had walked away or considered walking away from her marriage said that she was in deep emotional pain. If such pain is not decisively addressed, it can quickly spread, like an aggressive cancer, to the following five areas of your marriage.

1. *Trust.* It becomes harder to relax with your husband, and he no longer seems as dependable as he once was. You start to question his abilities, his actions, and his words.

2. *Dreams.* You stop making plans and lose interest in dreams you once shared. You might even have difficulty imagining your future together.

3. *Appreciation.* Personality traits and mannerisms that you once thought were positive lose their value—what charmed or excited you earlier now feels dull and boring. You might even find that you resent or despise what you once appreciated. It seems harder to see the good in your husband and the life you've built together.

4. *Libido.* Physical attraction to your husband fades, and interest in sexual connection of any kind is gone. His displays of affection become annoying or distasteful. You may come up with excuses to avoid any form of romance, or you may just go through the motions.

5. *Love.* Loving feelings are replaced with apathy and resentment. You might say you still love him or even have loving intentions, but you don't feel it. If you're honest with yourself, you might have to admit that you are so angry or disappointed that you don't have any tender feelings for him at all.

Cleaning House

In a way, emotional pain in a relationship is like dust in your house. For one thing, it's inevitable. For another, it can quickly build up if not taken care of on a regular basis. And when hurts settle on your marriage like dust on furniture, it doesn't really help to ignore them or complain how frequently you have to clean. But just as a dirty home doesn't mean you have to move, hurts don't mean you have to leave, either. What you have to do is clean house! That means facing the hurts honestly, without exaggeration or denial and, if possible, without blame. Here are four steps to get you started on this cleaning process.

1. *Pay attention to the source of your pain.* Your emotions are important, but they're not always accurate—and the fact that you're hurting doesn't necessarily mean your husband has done anything wrong. It's always possible that you've misunderstood him or that an innocent remark or action on his part has triggered your own insecurities. Your hurt may also be out of proportion to the offense because of some unresolved issue from your family of origin or a previous relationship that is unrelated to your marriage.

When you are feeling hurt, it's always a good idea to think a little before you respond to your feelings. Consider: "Is this an important issue to me?" Ask yourself: "Is this about him, or is it about me?"

2. *Choose to let go of minor hurts.* Even if your husband is responsible for your hurt, not every pain is worth a confrontation. Your husband is human and therefore is bound to annoy and disappoint you in many small ways. You do this to him as well. You can relieve yourself of a lot of pain if you simply accept that little hurts are part of any relationship and try not to take them personally. If you allow yourself to be disheartened about all the little things, your life will be miserable. It just makes sense to let go of as much as you can.

When you make the choice to let go of a hurt, however, make sure you really let it go. It's not fair to warehouse your hurts, only to bring them out later as weapons. If something has hurt you enough to store in your memory, it's better to deal with it directly and as soon as possible.

3. *Forgive the more significant hurts.* We know that forgiveness is not easy, especially when the hurts are deep or ongoing. Forgiving your husband can feel like giving up a part of yourself. But it's hard to underestimate the power of forgiveness in a marriage. It can be a source of wonderful freedom because when you choose to forgive, you release new energy and vitality in yourself. It also provides a model of how you want your husband to respond to you when you stumble or fall. And perhaps the best reasons for forgiving are that God asks us to do so and because He has forgiven us first: "Be kind to one another, tender-hearted, forgiving each other, just as God in Christ also has forgiven you."[4]

How do you forgive your husband? The sidebar on pages 98–9 outlines a process we have found helpful. We'll also have more to say about forgiveness in chapter 16. In the meantime, keep in mind that harboring bitterness and anger toward your husband hurts you more than it hurts him. It also undermines your marriage relationship and can harm your connection with God. No matter what you eventually decide about your marriage, the path of forgiveness is the only dependable path to peace.

4. *Give him a chance to repair the hurt.* Sometimes your husband will hurt you unintentionally. Other times, he intentionally lashes out because of his own pain. Either way, don't keep him in the dark about the fact that you are hurting. Try not to accuse or blame, but help him understand how deeply his actions have affected you. Tell him specifically what he can do to help you heal and move on—whether this means an apology, an act of restitution, or a serious plan showing how he can avoid repeating the pain he has caused.

This last point will require some thought on your part—which is why the first is so important. Before you can help your husband understand what he has done and how the damage can be repaired, you need to understand it yourself. There's no harm in waiting a little while to address the issue while you are thinking things through—but don't let thinking become an excuse or substitute for resolving the problem.

Step #1: *Face the hurt.* This may sound strange, but the first step toward forgiving another person is actually to admit how hurt and angry you really are.

Step #2: *Talk it out.* Explain your perspective and feelings as calmly as you can, and invite your husband to do the same—then listen. Seeing his side may not reduce the pain, but it can soften your heart and help you forgive.

Step #3: *Remember why forgiveness matters.* Jesus wants you to forgive others—not necessarily because they deserve it, not even because forgiving is good for you (though it is), but because He forgave you first.

Step #4: *Choose forgiveness.* This means you make a decision of the will, deliberately giving up your right to make your husband pay for the hurts he has caused.

Step #5: *Put the hurt behind you.* Forgetting isn't necessary—and may not be possible—but you need to stop rehearsing the pain over and over again. When memories arise (they will), choose to put them away and focus on other things.

Step #6: *Be patient with the process.* Forgiveness is rarely a simple, one-time proposition. If you've been deeply hurt, you might have to go through the whole process more than once. With God's help, you'll get there—and your reward will be peace and freedom.

Step #7: *Forgive yourself.* It's hard to forgive others if you can't forgive yourself. Even when you feel the guilt-producing secrets you carry in your heart are too horrible for forgiveness, extend to yourself the same grace you are trying to extend to your husband—the same grace God has already extended to you.[5]

The Four *A*s

Sometimes your hurt is so great that it seems impossible to ignore or forgive, and repair seems out of the question. There are hurts that feel like such overwhelming betrayals that you want to run as fast as you can and never look back. As we explained in chapter 1, we believe the most painful of these hurts stem from "the four *A*s"—abandonment, abuse, addictions, and adultery. These significant situations are frequently and understandably the ones that become marriage breakers.

Your personal history and past hurts will influence your ability to work through any one of the four *A*s—and of course your response will differ depending on which *A* is the problem and whether you or your husband is the "offender." In the material to come, we will assume that your husband is the one who has hurt you, but keep in mind that wives can commit these deep injuries against their husbands as well. (See chapter 14 for some help with such situations.)

The key question in whether your marriage can recover from one of the four *A*s will be whether your husband is hard-hearted or soft-hearted in regard to what he has done. We're not talking here about hard-hearted men as cruel and heartless or soft-hearted men as pushovers. We're talking about the depth of a man's repentance and the strength of his commitment to change.

Hard-hearted men are basically self-absorbed and tend to excuse, justify, or brag about their actions. Although they may experience periods of guilt and regret and sincerely pledge to "do better," their commitment to change is just not strong enough to overcome entrenched patterns, especially those of addiction and abuse.

A man whose heart has been softened, however, will be deeply repentant and committed to change, especially after he understands how he has hurt you. He will strongly desire to be a giving, loving, healthy husband. A husband whose heart is soft will mourn deeply over his failures and the pain he has caused. And he will have more than good intentions, promises, and apologies. He will do whatever it takes to win you back.

It's not always easy to know whether a man's heart has truly been softened. In the four *A* situations, therefore, we would urge you to be careful about trusting too quickly. Try to keep your heart open to the possibility of change, but give yourself time to observe whether the good intentions are dependable. In addition, because you are so emotionally involved with your husband and his struggles, you really need someone with wisdom and experience to guide you and help you keep perspective.

If confronted with any of the four *A*s in your marriage, we suggest that you immediately meet with a pastor or other spiritual advisor, and then, if at all possible, consult a counselor or trained professional to develop a plan for handling the situation. (If the problem is abuse and you feel that you and your children are in actual physical danger, the first thing you need to do is leave the house and find a safe place—even a police or fire station—before proceeding further.)

What you do next will depend on your personal situation and your counselor's advice, but one possibility is to write a firm letter to your husband that specifically articulates what the offense is and its impact on your marriage. Include in this letter what you need to see your husband do in order to deal with his personal issues and acknowledge the damage he has caused to the relationship. Since any of the four *A*s breaks the trust in a relationship, healing can't take place unless he first acknowledges the seriousness of what he has done.

In this letter you will need to include specific actions that will become indicators of whether or not he is willing to change. If the betrayal is abandonment (either physical, financial, or emotional), what must he do to prove to you that he is willing to reattach to you with love and gentleness? If the betrayal is abuse, what is he willing to do in terms of joining an anger management group, seeking professional help, exploring the root causes of his problem, and/or separating until the abuse issues are resolved to the point where there is no danger? If the problem is an addiction, what is he willing to do to commit to long-term involvement in a group, program, or plan to insure a lifetime of abstinence in his area of addiction? If the problem is an affair, what is he willing to do to make sure this never happens again? Will he break off *all* contact with the individual, set up an accountability person, recommit to the marriage and rebuild the basic trust that any healthy relationship needs?

Your husband's response to this letter and his willingness to respond to your specific requests will give you an idea whether you can move forward with the relationship. Even then, you will need the support of a counselor and loving friends to carry you through the process of healing.

Although any one of the four *A*s places you in a very difficult situation, please try to stay open to the possibility of change. We know your life is being torn apart, and it would be easy for you to close your heart as protection against further hurt. You need to be wise and realistic, but closing your heart completely also closes the door to hope.

We know many marriages that have survived the overwhelming pain of betrayal, allowing love and trust to grow again into something beautiful. We also know marriages in which one partner was so entrenched in his behavior that the other felt she had no choice but to leave. Our hearts ache for those who have experienced the excruciating pain of abandonment, abuse, addictions, or adultery. Without a miracle, some marriages seem too broken for fixing, but many others can survive if the husband and wife sincerely commit together to overcome hurts.

The soul would have no rainbow had the eyes no tears.

JOHN VANCE CHENEY

Running Away

In our experience of helping couples, we have found that healing unattended hurts is the most difficult part of restoring relationships. But no matter how difficult the process may be, it is almost always a better choice than just walking out. Unresolved hurts cling to your heart even when you think you are running away from them.

Natalie was working through a deep hurt in her marriage. On this particular day she looked tired, the strain showing on her face. "Have you ever thought about walking away?" I (Steve) asked.

She blushed and mumbled that she didn't know. I sat quietly, giving her time to process, not pushing, as tears gathered in her eyes and spilled down her cheeks. After a few minutes, she asked, "What would you think if I said yes?"

"Have your children ever thought about running away?"

At this she smiled a little. "Yes, don't all children think about it at one time or the other?"

"I think you're right," I said. "And probably most women think about it too. But kids don't get very far before they realize that running away creates more problems than it solves. Oh, they might go as far as packing a bag and even walking to the end of the street. But once they sit down and think it through for a while, they usually come back home."

I saw Natalie draw in a deep breath and let it out slowly before she answered. "Well, I've thought about leaving, and I've come to the same conclusion as my kids. Running away sounds good; but when it starts getting dark and you feel lonely, home has its advantages."

Something to Try

You can choose just one...

- Think back to some of the painful events in your childhood and teen years. Consider if any of these events might be influencing how you feel about your marriage lately.

- List three minor hurts you need to release.

_____

_____

_____

What is blocking you from letting go of them?

- List three more significant hurts you need to forgive.

_____

_____

_____

What is blocking you from forgiving?

- Sometime this week, when you are with a good friend, talk about the times in your life (childhood through present) when you felt like running away. Ask her if she had similar experiences, and then discuss how you felt, what brought on the feeling, how long it lasted, and what the results were.

Chapter 8

I'm So Mad I Could...

Anger is a thorn in the heart.

YIDDISH PROVERB

n our early years of marriage, one of the ways I (Alice) would handle arguments with my husband was to "punish" him with an angry outburst of my most hurtful words. Then, before Al could answer, I would slam the front door, get in the car, and drive away. Sometimes I drove for hours, never intending to go back. Now, some thirty years later, I wonder what people thought when they heard tires squealing around the corner and looked up to see the contorted face of a young blond woman screaming at her windshield.

Once my anger settled down, I headed back home and we would talk. There were times when it was difficult to figure out what had triggered such an angry outburst. Usually the argument started over something trivial, and the next thing I knew I was out of control and rehashing a string of past hurts. Resentment had smoldered in my heart and then, in an instant, released a spark of emotion that set my anger on fire.

Understanding Anger

Like other emotions, anger by itself is neither good nor bad. It just is. God gave us the emotion of anger to warn us when something threatens our physical or emotional well-being. Anger stimulates the production of adrenaline, enabling us to defend ourselves or run away.

Bestselling authors Gary Smalley and John Trent describe it this way:

> When a person becomes angry, his body goes on "full alert." When the inner brain gets the message that there is a stressful situation out there, it doesn't ask questions—it reacts. Your body can easily release as many chemicals and disrupt as many bodily functions when you are angry with your spouse as if you're being attacked by a wild animal.[1]

The anger response that Smalley and Trent describe can be a positive force, providing the energy and motivation we need to make necessary changes in our lives. But that same anger, if handled poorly, can easily become destructive. It can cause us to lash out and hurt others or be turned inward in the form of depression. It can spin out of control and cause us to do things we later regret. Or it can simmer inside and make us physically ill. Worst of all, it can cause us to shut the door of our love against the one we are supposed to love best.

Warning Signs of Anger

Do you have trouble even knowing you are angry? (Many women do.) Here are some important signs to watch out for.

- Do sarcastic remarks or swear words just "slip out"?

- Do you often feel physically tense or experience rapid heart rate, cold hands, jaw pain, or clenched teeth?

- Do other people complain that you answer them abruptly?

- Do you frequently find yourself sighing or feeling depressed?

- Are your kids or your husband constantly doing something wrong?

- Do your family or friends frequently ask, "Why are you so upset?"

- Have you ever broken anything in anger?

- Do you often perceive that other people are angry at you?[2]

Because many Christians see only the dark side of anger, they deny that they are struggling with it. Instead, they wrap their emotions in more acceptable words like *confused, stressed, irritated, frustrated,* or *misunderstood.* They may just grit their teeth, smile, and proclaim that everything is fine. They may even fool themselves to the point that they can't even *feel* their own anger. The trouble is, ignoring anger or pretending it doesn't exist won't make it go away; it simply drives it underground until it erupts in some inappropriate way—as a furious explosion, a passive-aggressive ploy, or even a stroke or heart attack.

When the apostle Paul warns, "Be angry, and yet do not sin; do not let the sun go down on your anger, and do not give the devil an opportunity,"[3] he doesn't mean we should try to keep it all pent up inside. Anger needs to be managed, not denied and buried, not blasted in the face of innocent bystanders, and certainly not unleashed in full destructive force on our husbands and our marriage vows.

The Four Horsemen

In his book *Why Marriages Succeed or Fail,* John Gottman writes about four responses to anger that can destroy the heart of a marriage. He calls them "the four horsemen of the apocalypse."[4] As you read the following summary of the four horsemen, remember that each one adds to the cycle of negativity and makes your relationship more and more unsatisfying.

Criticism. You attack the person rather than the difficulty. You blame your husband for your unhappiness, belittling his personality, character, or behavior.

Contempt. You dwell on negative thoughts about your husband, which stem from a disrespectful or disgusted attitude. Contempt can show itself in name-calling, mockery, rolling your eyes, or a sarcastic tone of voice.

Defensiveness. You emotionally withdraw to protect yourself. You deny personal responsibility for any misunderstandings or hurt in the relationship and make excuses for anything that might be perceived as your part. When your husband points out his own hurt or anger, you discount it and see it as his problem or attack again with more criticism and contempt.

Stonewalling. You either won't respond to him, or you respond with curt, single-word replies. You create emotional and/or physical distance. You keep your silence, and if he tries to break through, you ignore him or push him away.

I (Steve) asked one of my clients to read the list of horsemen and tell me which one she used the most. She laughed and said, "You got me, Dr. Steve. I'm good at all four of these…but I'm best at criticism and contempt. My husband is better at the other two."

"What if I told you that criticism and contempt in one partner frequently leads to defensiveness and stonewalling in the other?" I asked.

"Are you saying that I'm making the situation worse?"

"What I suggest is to stop attacking your husband. Try to be more positive and show him appreciation and respect. You might find that he starts opening up."

What to Do with Anger

Every couple will have their moments when anger flares up. Just as a smoldering fire can be dampened or inflamed, you can handle your anger with water or gasoline. Too often in the stress of the moment, we make the situation worse by using a bucket of four-horsemen gasoline.

What's the alternative to either stuffing our anger or handling it in destructive four-horsemen fashion? Here are some steps to help you manage anger in a healthy way.

Delay briefly. This doesn't mean putting it off until next week, but take a brief time out to cool off. Try stepping outside for a few minutes and taking some deep breaths. Walk around the block, pray, journal your feelings. Thomas Jefferson gave wise advice when he said, "When angry, count to ten. When very angry, count to one hundred."

Get perspective. Although anger is a natural response to hurt or fear, it isn't always an *accurate* response to the event that triggered it. You can be honestly angry and still be wrong about what happened. So while you're counting to ten it's a good idea to mentally back off a little and try to get perspective. Did your husband intentionally goad you, or was it an oversight or a careless word? Did you contribute to the problem? Are you really angry with someone besides your husband? Calling a friend can give you added perspective—but make it a friend who will be honest and not just agree with you.

Nicole Johnson, an actress and popular speaker who

travels nationally with the Women of Faith conferences, found that it was useful to interview herself whenever she felt angry. She would ask questions like: What happened? What am I fearful of? Where have my feelings been hurt? Why am I frustrated?[5] Answering these questions honestly not only gave her needed perspective, but also clarified the steps she needed to take to deal with it in a healthy way.

Decide if you need to talk. If your anger is related to your husband or your relationship, it's important to bring the matter up for discussion with him. If you realize you're really angry with someone else—including yourself or God—that's the person you need to talk with. If you realize you're angry over a situation that cannot be changed, your wiser choice might be to work out the energy of your anger through vigorous exercise or some other kind of self-expression. A long, brisk walk or a half hour with your journal can be remarkably helpful in calming your anger and helping you understand what steps to take next.

Talk it out carefully. Once you have decided you need to share your angry feelings with your husband, watch your tone of voice and your body language. Remember the four horsemen—a whining or sarcastic tone is hard to listen to without becoming defensive. The Bible says that a soft or gentle answer turns away wrath.[6] Using a soft tone helps you express your anger without injuring the other person.

It's also important to keep focused when expressing your anger to your husband. One man said, "When I have an argument with my wife, she doesn't get hysterical; she gets historical." It is important to limit your discussion to the current situation instead of bringing up past disappointments. Focus on the actions that caused the immediate problem, not on your husband as a person. It will help if you avoid phrases like, "you always," "you never," and "you are just like." These types of words tend to trigger defensiveness and are seldom completely true.

No matter what you say, try to concentrate on healing, not hurting. It's important to be honest when sharing your angry feelings, but the goal should never be to wound the other person. Try to listen to your husband's response without becoming defensive or defeated. Expressing anger in a healthy way is a learned skill, and you will get better at it the more you practice.

End well. Try to end the discussion with a word of kindness or reach out and touch your husband in a way that expresses acceptance and peace. A pastor's wife, Joyce Fischer, explained that it can take hours before you feel like *ending well.* Sometimes while lying stiffly in bed on her side of the mattress, she would realize she hadn't reached out in kindness. She found that the simple act of brushing her big toe across her husband's ankle served as her signal of peace.

Open Hand and Open Heart

In their "Love Is a Decision" seminar, authors Gary Smalley and John Trent use a wonderful visual to show the importance of handling anger well in a marriage. They suggest holding your hand up, palm open, fingers spread wide apart. An open hand represents an open heart ready to reach out to others—including your husband. Fingers that are wiggling mean you are happy and everything is healthy in a relationship.

Smalley and Trent go on to explain that when you are hurt, your heart begins to close and you are no longer eager to reach out for love. To demonstrate this, they suggest slowly closing your hand. As your fingers tighten all the way, you have a closed fist—the worldwide symbol of anger and defiance. When hurtful words and actions are allowed to grow into bitter anger—and when anger is either stuffed or allowed to run amok—the result is a defensive, closed heart.[7]

In this broken world, it is impossible to avoid anger. If you find it erupting in your own heart, ask the hard questions to discover what caused the outburst. Then deal with it immediately—not days or weeks later. Spend time on your knees asking God to uncurl your heart as you would uncurl the fingers of a closed fist. With open hand and open heart, reach out to the one you once loved deeply. When anger is dealt with and hurts are healed, you'll find you can love him deeply again.

Something to Try

You can choose just one...

- What do you think triggers anger in your husband? What does your husband do that triggers your anger?

- Draw a picture that represents your anger.

- Review the six steps to help manage anger found in this chapter. Which ones are you already doing? Which ones do you need to work on improving?

- Likewise, review the four responses to anger that John Gottman calls "the four horsemen of the apocalypse." Identify which "horseman" you tend to use the most. Which one does your husband use the most?

- Linda Douglas writes, "To apologize, I buy a cake at a bakery and have them frost "Sorry" on it. No one can resist it."[8] Maybe you can try this the next time you know you should apologize.

Chapter 9

This Lady Has the Blues

*I can look back at my darkest periods
and realize that these were the times
when the Lord was holding me closest.
But I couldn't see his face because my face
was in his breast crying.*

JOHN MICHAEL TALBOT

t's two o'clock on a beautiful summer afternoon, and I (Steve) have an unexpected free hour before seeing my next client. As I begin this chapter, I'm thinking about Christine, who started seeing me a little over a month ago. Even though my office is warm and inviting, she spent most of her first visit gripping the arms of one of my overstuffed chairs as if bracing herself for a terrifying roller-coaster ride. Today, she seemed much more relaxed. Kicking off her shoes and tucking her feet beneath her, Christine was eager to talk about the progress in her battle with depression.

Although recent research shows at least one out of four women will struggle with depression during her lifetime, many are reluctant to seek the help they so desperately need. Perhaps the word *depression* sounds scary. Maybe women worry about what other people will think, or they just don't understand their symptoms and hope they'll go away. But depression, like many other real problems, tends to become worse if left untreated. One woman who delayed getting help described her symptoms this way. "Have you ever had one of those days when it takes tremendous effort just to drag your body out of bed? I had 'one of those days,' and it lasted for months."[1]

As mentioned in earlier chapters, unresolved marriage problems can and often do lead to depression. Depression, in turn, can cause or exacerbate marital difficulties—and rob you of the energy you need to work on them effectively. In fact, it is so common for walk-out women to be depressed that the very desire to leave can be thought of as a symptom of depression.

If you are experiencing loss of energy, poor concentration, disinterest in friends and work, altered appetite and sleep, anxiety, or a sense of hopelessness, you may have this debilitating condition—especially if your symptoms have lasted for two weeks or longer. Depression is treatable, and I urge you to seek professional help for an evaluation.

Does the very idea make you uneasy? Perhaps the next few pages can help.

For the rest of this chapter, I'll put on my psychologist's hat and give you a glimpse of three counseling sessions. If you, like Christine, came to me with symptoms of depression, the following might be some of what we would talk about. I hope that reading through this will remove some of your anxiety. Remember as you read, however, that every situation calls for unique treatment. I am not offering a "fix-all" formula, but a general picture of how depression can affect your life and also how it might be handled. So lean back into one of my cozy overstuffed chairs, take a deep breath, and relax.

The Color of Blue

During the first appointment, I spend a great deal of time listening—listening much deeper than your words. I listen for emotions, fears, hurts, and frustration. When you say that you feel stuck or trapped, I try to understand what has caused you to feel that way. Often in my practice, I notice that this stuck feeling brings with it the blues—that unwelcome emotion that wraps you in a wet blanket and leaves you feeling low and unhappy.

There are two kinds of feeling blue—two varieties of depression. What I call *light blue* is a hazy shade of melancholy that seems to surround you. The excitement is gone, and life doesn't seem as good as it once did. You continue doing the things you need to do, but the joy is gone. Oh, maybe there are some days when you break free of the dullness and life seems great for a while, but just as quickly the sun disappears again behind the clouds and you feel disconnected and discontent.

Then there's the *dark blue* that sends chills of depression deep into your heart. There are no days when the sun breaks through, and soon you begin to feel helpless and hopeless. If this situation is left unchecked, you can get caught in what psychologists call a "depressive triad"— believing that things are bad, they have always been bad, and they always will be bad.

Because I want to understand just how depressed you are feeling, I'll begin asking questions about different areas of your life.

Emotions: How stuck do you feel? How hurt or angry are you? How often do you cry or wish you could cry?

Thoughts: What sorts of ideas go through your mind these days? Do you find it difficult to concentrate or remember things?

Actions: How has this stuck feeling affected your everyday activities? What has it done to your motivation? Do you complete most tasks you begin?

Body: Is there a change in your appetite or sleep patterns? Are you experiencing headaches, stomachaches, or any other kind of physical pain?

Relationships: How do you feel about the people you once cared for the most? Are you more withdrawn, critical, or argumentative?

Faith: How close do you feel to God? Do you feel distant and want to hide? Or do you want to run to Him?

Knowing how severe your symptoms are will help me determine who besides me should come alongside to help you. If you are hurt and want to withdraw, you need good friends. If your blues are keeping you from God, you need your pastor or a spiritual mentor. If your overall depression is strong, you probably also need a physician to evaluate you for physical causes and treatment as well as a counselor.

Possible Triggers of Depression

Unresolved childhood issues	Grief, loss, or rejection
Parenting stress	Past or current traumas
Financial difficulties	Unforgivingness
Family history of depression	Guilt
Medical conditions	Personal failure
Hormone imbalance	Job-related pressures
Weight issues	Identity confusion
High stress sensitivity	Poor self-care
Chronic pain	Repressed anger
Social pressure	Low self-esteem
Negative thinking and rumination	Marital issues

What Triggers the Blues?

After we talk about the two types of depression, I want us both to get a clear and honest picture of how you are feeling, so I'll ask you to share with me all the reasons you can think of that might have triggered your current case of the blues. Sometimes the causes of depression can be something internal, like a biochemical or hormonal imbalance. Other times it can be caused by external pressures, like relationships or finances. Depression doesn't often fit neatly into a box but is messy and spills over into a combination of boxes. Your blues may be triggered by any number of circumstances—a list of possibilities is found on page 121. I usually try to identify two or three as the most likely.

In looking at the sidebar, you'll notice that marriage issues are at the bottom of the list. This is intentional because I don't want you to jump to the conclusion that your husband is the cause of your depression. When you feel down and discouraged, you tend to blame those who are the closest to you and so, by default, your husband might become the primary suspect. But even though he probably has a lot of areas in which he needs to improve— most of us do—you can't automatically assume that he is the primary cause of your blues.

By the end of our first "appointment," you are likely feeling better. Just the opportunity to talk in a deep, more directed way seems to lighten the heaviness of the blues. As you get ready to leave, I promise you that I will be persistent and patient with you if you will be persistent and patient with yourself. I can sense you stiffen a little when I ask you to write down a homework assignment, but I know you will relax and maybe even smile when you see the last item. Here's the assignment I give you:

List any triggers we didn't talk about.

Get together with a supportive, empathetic friend and share how you are feeling.

Do something special for yourself every day! (This should be something you really enjoy—not something you "should" do.)

At this point, our time together is through. As you rise to leave, I remind you that even though things look dark, you're going to make it through this difficult time. I urge you to hang on to hope as you struggle with your depression. It is important for you to realize that change rarely happens in giant, life-rattling leaps. Usually it occurs in small, unsteady steps—a few steps forward and then some back. The apostle Paul says that suffering builds patience, patience builds character, and character builds hope.[2] Your blues will probably not disappear as quickly as you wish, but if you are patient, changes will happen deep in your heart, and this will ultimately lead to a richer, more fulfilling life than you could possibly imagine.

123

Weeping may remain for a night,
but rejoicing comes in the morning.

PSALM 30:5, NIV

Highs and Lows

When you return for your second appointment, I can see that you are feeling more comfortable than the last time, and this pleases me. I'll lean back, probably cross one leg over my knee, and ask you how you felt about your homework. I'm interested not only in what you did, but also what you didn't do and why. So we talk about your lowest points and the fact that your depression is causing you to avoid physical activity, social involvement, and things that used to be fun.

One thing that catches my attention is that your conversation is punctuated with comments like "Who wants to be with someone who is depressed?" "When I feel better, I'll get more active," and "Why waste money trying to have fun when all it's going to do is make me feel more miserable?" This concerns me because I believe that such negative statements can become self-fulfilling and because the more passive and isolated you become, the deeper blue you will feel. I make a note to spend some time next week discussing how to turn your negative self-talk around. For now, however, I simply encourage you to spend the next week doing some specific activities you are resisting.

First, since it has been more than a year since your last complete physical, I want you to schedule one as soon as possible. In addition, look over the following assignment and do at least one activity in each category:

Social: I urge you to invite a girlfriend for lunch or coffee, attend a function where there are people you know, go to church, or choose another activity that involves being with other people.

Active: I encourage you to reduce passive activities such as reading, napping, and television and replace them with

124

active ones such as walking, swimming, or aerobics—anything that will get you out of the house and get your adrenaline flowing.

Fun: Think through all the things that used to be fun and choose one to do again. It can be as simple as taking a ride on a merry-go-round or as creative as putting together a new layout for your scrapbook. You don't have to "feel like" doing it; just do it.

Health: Finally, I urge you to try to get at least seven hours of sleep each night, reduce sweets, avoid excess caffeine, and to substitute healthful snacks like fruit or unsalted nuts for junk food.

Before you leave, I want you to understand that getting started will be the hardest part of the homework. I know that you might be discouraged because you didn't do as well as you wanted on last week's assignment. But this week's assignments are designed to energize you rather than drain you. I can see doubt in your eyes, but I ask that you just trust me on this one.

Reversing the Downward Cycle

When you come in for your third appointment, you are quite pleased that you did three homework activities— social, active, and fun—all at once by inviting a friend to go with you to play golf.

Good for you! I'm proud of you. You've made a lot of progress.

Now I want to spend some time talking about your positive and negative influences. When you are feeling blue, everything around you looks dark; it's like looking at the world through a pair of sunglasses. This negative viewpoint influences your attitude, the way you talk to yourself, and the way you treat others. And your negative attitude, in turn, affects the way you look at the world. Soon you can't even see the bright side of life, and everything seems hopeless.

To reverse the downward spiral, it's important to maximize the positive and minimize the negative by clearing out as many negative influences as possible. I want you to look through your days and remove anything that exacerbates your dark mood—television programs, books, music, events, thought patterns, and even people.

An accumulation of the negative reminds me of my son's bedroom. If he leaves sweaty socks, damp towels, and dirty shirts in the corner, after a few weeks the room develops a certain earthy odor. Just like he needs to clean out his room, you need to stop hanging around negative people (if possible) and also stop turning on negative media and listening to depressing music.

Yet cleaning out is only the beginning. Jesus warns about getting rid of something negative without filling the place with something good. When He talked about casting out an evil spirit, Jesus said, "So it returns and finds that its former home is all swept and clean. Then the spirit finds seven other spirits more evil than itself, and they all enter the person and live there."[3] As this graphic illustration shows, it's important to replace the negative with something good and positive. So I urge you to surround yourself with positive people, books, music, and atmosphere.

At this point, we'll also chat about what I call "self-talk." I'll encourage you to make positive statements to yourself even if you don't fully believe them—because the words you say can really change the way you think. I may even suggest some positive things for you to tell yourself the next week. This idea of positive self-talk comes right from the Bible. The apostle Paul puts it this way: "Fix your thoughts on what is true and honorable and right. Think about things that are pure and lovely and admirable. Think about things that are excellent and worthy of praise."[4] By repeating positive statements to yourself, you are really following Paul's advice.

By now you're looking doubtful, so I assure you that I understand that developing an upbeat attitude isn't as easy as it sounds. It's not just a matter of funneling in some positive input. The truth is, some people are naturally more optimistic and therefore more resistant to the blues. For them, thinking positively and shaking off the blues is easier. For others it is a much more difficult process. Nevertheless, positive thinking really can foster positive feelings, so I urge you not to give up—and I give you an assignment that will help.

One day at a time, for one week, I want you to practice thinking like an optimist. Do all you can to see every glass half full and in every cloud look for the silver lining.

If negative thoughts occur, deliberately argue them down with a positive perspective. Write out what you discover, and talk about it with your husband or a friend. When we get together again, I'll look forward to hearing about how being an optimist for a week has changed your overall attitude.

There is so much more I want to know about you and your individual struggle with depression. My prayers go with you on those dark days when you feel so lonely and discouraged that you want to walk away from everything. I know I can't fully understand your pain and struggle, but I too have had my dark days when all seemed hopeless—and I survived. So have countless women I have known. So in the midst of your difficulties, please remember that you are not alone and that God can provide a way out of every darkness.

God gave a special blessing to encourage the children of Israel as they wandered for forty years in a dry and desolate wilderness, no doubt experiencing the same kind of discouragement that drags you down. Let this same blessing be my prayer for you as you struggle with a long, hard bout of the blues and fight for the survival of your marriage in the midst of it.

> May the LORD bless you and protect you.
> May the LORD smile on you and be gracious to you.
> May the LORD show you his favor and give you
> his peace.[5]

Something to Try

You can choose just one...

- Write out how you would describe your "light blue" moods. Do the same for your "dark blue" moods, if you have them.

- Look at the list of possible depression triggers on page 121, and circle the ones that have affected you the most. What has worked in the past to help you overcome these triggers? What has made them worse?

- Try to think of at least one woman you know who struggles with the blues. Review the ideas for activities on pages 124–5, and consider how you might encourage her to do something uplifting.

- Time to pamper yourself. Enjoy a leisurely bath, an invigorating walk, tea with a friend—or splurge on a pedicure or massage.

Chapter 10

Different Walls

*Before I built a wall
I'd ask to know what I was
walling in or walling out.*

ROBERT FROST, "MENDING WALL"

a few years back, I (Alice) discovered a deeply touching poem by Richard A. McCray. I would like to quote it here in its entirety because it describes so vividly what it's like when two people who once loved each other grow apart. According to a brief introduction by the poet, it depicts something that happened in his own marriage:

Walls

*Their wedding picture mocked them from the table,
these two whose minds no longer touched each other.
They lived with such a heavy barricade between them
that neither battering ram of words
nor artilleries of touch could break it down.*

*Somewhere, between the oldest child's first tooth
and the youngest daughter's graduation,
they lost each other.*

Throughout the years each slowly unraveled
that tangled ball of string called self,
and as they tugged at stubborn knots,
each hid his searching from the other.

Sometimes she cried at night and
begged the whispering darkness to tell her who she was.
He lay beside her, like a hibernating bear,
unaware of her winter.

Once, after they had made love,
he wanted to tell her how afraid he was of dying,
but, fearful to show his naked soul,
he spoke instead of the beauty of her breasts.

She took a course on modern art,
trying to find herself in colors splashed upon a canvas,
complaining to the other women about men
who are insensitive.

He climbed into a tomb called "The Office,"
wrapped his mind in a shroud of paper figures,
and buried himself in customers.

Slowly, the wall between them rose, cemented by
the mortar of indifference.

One day, reaching out to touch each other,
they found a barrier they could not penetrate,
and recoiling from the coldness of the stone,
each retreated from the stranger on the other side.

For when love dies, it is not in a moment of angry battle,
nor when fiery bodies lose their heat.
It lies panting, exhausted,
expiring at the bottom of a wall it could not scale.[1]

Although the poem is beautifully written, reading it always leaves my heart feeling sad because I don't know what happened after these sorrowful words were penned. Mr. McCray dedicates the poem to his wife, so there is a reason to hope that the marriage was restored. I sometimes pray for the two of them, longing for them to be back together and happy in their marriage. If they are, I believe God is smiling because the wall they built eventually came tumbling down.

Wall Building

We have kept a set of small wooden blocks our children used for building when they were little. You know the kind—about one and three-quarters inches square with numbers and pictures painted on them. We used to love watching our children stack them row upon row. With careful coordination, the wall of blocks grew higher and higher, until, with the slightest tap, it came crashing down. Again and again the game was repeated until at last the blocks were put away. If the walls built between a husband and wife could be dismantled as easily, they would not be much of a problem. But in marriage, when barriers are left unattended over the months and years, they become tall, wide, thick, and strong.

Marriage walls start small—a single brick and then another, a thoughtless remark, a testy reply, a sigh of

133

frustration, a decision that working through a particular problem just isn't worth it. At first the wall seems so insignificant that you hardly notice it, or if you do, you can easily step right over it. However, trying to ignore it is the worst thing you can do, because unless the early layers are knocked down, the wall gets higher with each unresolved frustration or challenge. Before you realize it, it is so high you can't crawl over it, and soon you lose touch and sight of each other. One day, as the poem says, when you try to reach out and touch, you'll find the barrier cannot be penetrated. You're on different sides, leading more or less separate lives, with little in common and little to talk about.

When marriages reach this point, counselors call them "parallel marriages" or "emotional divorces." Others see the husband and wife as "married, but single." Whatever name they go by, it seems so tragic when a husband and wife who once loved spending many hours together now avoid each other as much as possible, separated by a wall one or both have built.

Why Build a Wall?

Very simply, a wall is for protection. We build walls and fences around our homes to keep our children safe inside and to keep dangerous intruders out. The same principle applies when we build walls in our marriages: We are walling something in and/or walling something out.

When you have been deeply wounded, it is difficult to continually expose yourself to hurt and disappointment, so the walls you build may be forms of self-protection. If you were mistreated as a child or in a previous relationship, you may be especially prone to withdrawing and gathering your feelings inside so your heart is protected from being hurt again. By locking your love and desire inside, you feel less vulnerable. Even if you long for emotional intimacy, you might be plagued by fearful thoughts: *If I let my guard down, he will disappoint me. I can't risk being hurt and going through the pain again.*

The risk of being hurt is a part of any relationship. Caution and concern are natural and may be necessary at times. But the walls you build to protect yourself can also trap you inside—stunting your growth, blocking your vision, and fueling your fear. Soon this fear becomes so strong that you start believing you cannot survive one more hurt.

Walling your husband out is a sincere attempt to protect yourself from this pain. But by walling your emotions safe inside, you lock your husband outside. You emotionally disengage, keeping distance between the two of you. This may cause tension, but you don't necessarily mind because tension helps the distance grow even wider. You might even be grateful for it since you lack the energy or desire to work on the relationship. However, this type of protection can set in place a pattern of events that numb you to love and can permanently separate you from your husband not only emotionally, but at every level.

One woman who responded to our marriage survey described her walls this way: "I've been hurt, angry, and disappointed for so long that I don't want to resolve problems. I just want to start over." When someone has been hurt this deeply, it is natural for her to reinforce the wall—adding more bricks and spreading extra mortar in the cracks—doing everything she can to keep her husband from reaching her heart.

Words That Build Walls

- I told you so.
- If you don't like it, you can just leave.
- That was stupid.
- Can't you do anything right?
- It's all your fault.
- What's wrong with you?
- You get what you deserve.
- I don't know why I stay married to you.

STEVE STEPHENS[2]

Mortar and Bricks

The beginning of wall building is often unintentional, but if you don't stop the process, the power of making it higher and stronger becomes almost addictive. If you are in the habit of blaming and complaining instead of reasoning and resolving, it is likely that you are feeding the addiction. You soon realize that building a wall isn't just to protect yourself; it is also a way of hurting your husband. You come to see him as the enemy—the cause of painful conflict, hurtful words, broken promises, belittling, criticism, and thoughtlessness—so you reach for the bricks and mortar. If you are wondering what kind of actions build walls, here are just a few examples:

Silence. You may deprive your husband of connecting with you by refusing to talk to him or, when he tries to talk to you, refusing to respond—or giving vague, evasive, fake answers. Inside, you may feel too worn out even to discuss the issue, you may tell yourself that he doesn't really care so there's no point in talking, or you may consciously be trying to punish him.

Coldness. You keep your husband at a distance by refusing to show him kindness, affection, or vulnerability. You may be openly rude or coldly polite, but either way, you lock your heart by not showing emotions—not even tears.

Sexual withdrawal. You seldom are "in the mood," and you deprive your husband of intimacy by avoiding physical connection, even touch. You may ignore him or belittle him if he doesn't approach you in the right way and at the right time—or you may just always have an excuse.

Intensity. Attacking, threatening, or manipulating your husband either verbally or nonverbally. This can be done with a glare, a certain tone of voice, or an aggressive body posture. Any way you send it, the message is clear: *Just stay away or you will regret it.*

Busyness. You may be preoccupied with hobbies, children's activities, work-related duties, and church responsibilities. You are rarely home when your husband is, and when you are, you just don't have time to connect with or give attention to him.

You may not be the only one building the wall, of course. In fact, you probably aren't the only one. Your husband is on the other side, adding his own bricks and mortar to wall himself in and keep you out.

The tragedy of this whole process is that the more the two of you try to protect yourselves, the more harm you are doing to each other and to your marriage. Whatever materials you use to build your walls—and however high they have grown—our hearts go out to you because you are avoiding all that will help your relationship and choosing instead what will destroy it. Although you are just trying to protect yourself, you are actually building a deadly trap that undermines communication and destroys hope.

If the wall between you continues to grow, before long it will cast a shadow over everything good in your relationship. If it is not torn down, it may ultimately end your marriage. What is a divorce but the final brick in the wall between two people? Just as tragic is when you remain together but the wall between you grows so thick that you have a marriage in name only—devoid of the support and intimacy that God intended for marriage.

Dismantling Walls

The good news when it comes to walls in your marriage is that in many ways it's easier to tear them down than it was to build them up. It's true that they didn't get built overnight, and they won't come down overnight either—but whatever effort it takes is more than worth it.

Sprinkled throughout this book are chapters with specific ideas about letting go of hurts, handling conflict, connecting again, nurturing your spirit, and dreaming new dreams. But here we want to briefly mention five specific strategies for tearing down walls—or better yet, keeping them from being built in the first place.

1. *Build your courage and your hope.* Because fear, hurt, and discouragement are the impetus behind most wall building, your first strategy for taking down your marital wall is to find more positive ways to cope with the negative emotions that drove you to build the walls in the first place. We urge you to develop resources to manage your negative feelings *before* taking them out on your husband. If you have persisted in praying for your husband through the past weeks, you have already begun this process. We urge you to pray for yourself as well and to seek the support of a loving friend or counselor.

One of the most helpful things you can do at this point

is to shift your attitude about your husband. You may be so accustomed to thinking of him as the enemy and the cause of all your problems that you've lost sight of the human being he really is. Or you may have been so caught up in your own needs and feelings that you've ignored his. As you continue to pray for your husband, ask God to help you reverse that attitude. Remind yourself frequently that he really is your all, and that you are on the same side.

> Trusting God is doing the greatest thing anybody can do.
>
> ELISABETH ELLIOT

Even more important, try to keep your heart open to the Lord. God knows that working through these difficult challenges will bring out the very best in you. He is there by your side, inviting you to lean hard on Him. In Psalm 46, the Lord asks us not to fear even if "the earth give way and the mountains fall" (NIV). Surely, He does not want us to fear when the mortar gives way and the walls fall. Can you open your heart to hear these precious words that God is speaking to you: "I am your refuge and your strength, an ever-present help in times of trouble"?[3]

2. *Establish some positive connections.* Even if you don't feel strong enough to knock down the wall between you and your husband, you can start the process by throwing some friendly messages over the wall. Make a point of cooking one of his favorite meals. Offer a back rub when he looks tired or stressed. Invite your husband to catch a movie and

press your knee against his. Say yes to his romantic overtures, even if you're not really in the mood. Little gestures like these may feel awkward or fake, but they are simple, nonthreatening ways to reestablish common ground between you and make some deposits in your love banks.

I (Steve) often tell my clients that feelings follow actions. When you act in loving ways toward your husband or even just respond to him in a friendly, positive manner, you establish connections that can grow into friendly or loving feelings. This doesn't mean that if you pretend you have a good marriage you will automatically develop one. But your efforts at establishing goodwill will almost always leave you feeling better about your husband and your relationship.

3. *Initiate a dialogue about what has happened in your marriage and what you would like to see happen.* There's no way around it: If you're going to dismantle the walls in your marriage, you eventually need to *talk* about the situation. If you can manage it, the best way is to approach this subject head-on. Tell your husband that you regret the distance that has grown between you, that you share the blame for this and would like to work with him to reverse the situation. Many of the communication techniques outlined in chapter 11 can be useful here.

4. *Set some safety rules.* Because walls are erected for self-protection, tearing them down can be very frightening. To reduce the risk, it's important to discuss ways you can make your marriage safer, more fulfilling, and more inviting for both of you. You cannot hint at these things; you must be

very specific about your needs in this regard. We suggest that you write down five specific things he can do in the next week that will help you feel safe—and ask him to do the same. Read your list to him and give him a fair chance to respond. Do the same for his list.

5. *Work on learning to trust each other again.* Once you've gotten this far, the rest of the process involves persistently chiseling at your walls of suspicion, fear, and mistrust brick by brick—and not putting up new bricks in the meantime. At the beginning, it will be hard for you to believe and accept the things your husband does right. He may be awkward in his approaches, and you may feel he is only doing them to trick you for a time or to get his own way. You may even wish subconsciously that he would keep acting like a jerk so you will be justified in walking out. But when your husband tries to fulfill your desires, it is extremely important that you accept even the little things he does. Remember that returning to love is a process that takes time, effort, and sacrifice for both of you.

A Story of Another Wall

As we write this chapter, it is our deepest prayer that you will begin to cherish your husband again—that you will be filled with admiration and love for him, that he will become the treasure of your heart. We hope the following story from medieval Germany, retold here by Rochelle M. Pennington, will inspire you.

The wives who lived within the walls of Weinsberg Castle in Germany were well aware of the riches it held: gold, silver, jewels, and wealth beyond belief.

Then the day came in 1141 A.D. when all their treasure was threatened. An enemy army had surrounded the castle wall and demanded the fortress, the fortune, and the lives of the men within. There was nothing to do but surrender.

Although the conquering commander had set a condition for the safe release of all women and children, the wives of Weinsberg refused to leave without having one of their own conditions met as well. They demanded that they be allowed to fill their arms with as many possessions as they could carry out with them. Knowing that the women couldn't possibly make a dent in the massive fortune, their request was honored.

When the castle gates opened, the army outside was brought to tears. Each woman had carried out her husband.

The wives of Weinsberg, indeed, were well aware of the riches behind the castle walls.[4]

Something to Try

You can choose just one...

- List the words or actions your husband uses that are most likely to cause you to build a wall.

- List the words or actions you use that are most likely to cause your husband to build a wall.

- Which phrase best describes the current wall between you and your husband?

  - It's very low and hardly noticeable.

  - No one else can see it, but we know it's there.

  - It's high enough that we run into it more often than we want to admit.

  - It's so high and wide that it is easier to avoid each other than to try and connect.

  - It's high, wide, and strong enough to make us feel like it isn't possible to tear down.

- Take the time to drive out into the countryside or hike to a place where there is a view. Breathe deeply and enjoy the feel of open spaces. Think about some of the best memories of your marriage.

Chapter 11

Let's Talk

The problem with communication in marriage is that every time the husband has words with his wife, she has paragraphs with him.

AUTHOR UNKNOWN

t was a cool January afternoon when Curt and Kari first came to my (Steve's) office. After seventeen years of marriage, Kari was ready to pack her bags and leave. Curt stared out the window as Kari explained that she was tired of scrambling to meet everyone's needs while her needs were being ignored. She felt like her husband wasn't capable of having a meaningful conversation and that he never paid attention when she talked to him.

At this point, Curt shifted his body so he was facing away from her. Finally in frustration Kari said, "There he goes again, refusing to listen to me."

Curt turned his head toward her and said, "What do you mean? This is how I always sit."

"I know," Kari retorted. "That's the problem."

Top of the List

When marriages start to crumble, poor communication is one of the reasons at the top of the list. In fact, most marriage counselors agree that good communication is foundational for a healthy marriage. And though there are many different ways to communicate, women usually feel the need for verbal dialogue. Willard F. Harley, author of *His Needs, Her Needs,* lists communication as a woman's number one basic need in marriage (the second is affection),[1] and we believe this is true. When women get together and talk about their marriage disappointments, one of the first things they mention is that "we just don't talk anymore"—or as an unhappy woman once wrote to columnist Ann Landers, that their marriages have grown dull, boring, and "out of conversation."[2]

But lack of conversation isn't the only communication difficulty that can plague a marriage. Sometimes there are plenty of words in a marriage, but they are so pointed and hurtful that they become part of the problem. Words can hurt, especially when they are spoken in anger. And even the most well-intentioned words can be misread, misinterpreted, or just ignored—especially in a troubled marriage where partners have grown wary.

Good News and Bad News

If poor, negative, or nonexistent communication is the primary reason your marriage is crumbling, we've got good news—and perhaps bad news as well. The good news is that poor communication is actually one of the easiest trouble spots in a marriage to repair. "Easiest" doesn't mean the repair won't take determination and effort. But there are some basic tools that can really improve this connection between husband and wife.

How could that be bad news? Often when a woman is thinking of giving up on her marriage, she resists improving communication. Deep in her heart, she knows that if she and her husband start talking on a healthy level, the improved communication will draw them closer together and will weaken her reasons for leaving. She doesn't trust words because she fears they may lure her back where she will be hurt again.

Even if that is true for you, the bad news can be changed to good if you give it a chance. Start by trying to remember a time when you thought your husband's conversation was irresistible or at least appealing. (If you felt that way before, you can feel that way again.) And then, before reading any further, take a minute to ponder two questions:

- What's it like being married to me?
- What's it like hearing the words I say?

Whenever I (Alice) feel like my Al is disappointing me in some way, I try to ask myself those two questions. Most of the time I realize I've been so focused on *his* few shortcomings that I've overlooked how much *my* actions are contributing to the problem. And this certainly applies to our communication glitches—those times when we just aren't connecting with each other.

I encourage women to ask these questions on a regular basis. Not only are they good for a quick attitude adjustment; they can also give us a fresh perspective on why communication with our husbands is less than satisfactory. Sometimes husbands close down their communication because of the way they are being treated. When wives get negative, picky, sarcastic, or hurtful, men tend to tune out or become defensive and argumentative. There may even be times when they give up and stop talking all together.

When communication is a problem in a marriage, it's rarely one person's fault entirely. Personality styles, gender differences, ethnic background, and personal issues can all contribute to misunderstandings. But a little bit of empathy, along with some effort at changing the ways you speak and listen, can do a lot to make your relationship both more interesting and more peaceful.

> *Marriage is sewn together by ten thousand tiny stitches.*
> *It's within the context of these little communications*
> *that we begin to work out the major issues of life.*
>
> THOMAS KINKADE[3]

Watch What You Say

Words have incredible power. With them we can praise, affirm, and encourage, or we can hurt, humiliate, and destroy. Surely that is why the apostle Paul wrote, "Do not let any unwholesome talk come out of your mouths, but only what is helpful for building others up according to their needs."[4] Simply put: Negative communication can pull a marriage apart.

If you are like most women who are considering walking out, unhealthy talk may be par for the course in your marriage. Frustration and hostility probably spill over into your words and even the spaces between your words. At a time when a positive connection is most needed, the following "unwholesome" communication habits can build walls instead of bridges:[5]

Negative statements. Few things kill a relationship faster than ridicule, insults, name-calling, or criticism. Negativity isn't limited to words. A condescending tone of voice, a roll of the eyes, a contemptuous look—all can communicate scorn or disapproval. For people who require verbal affirmation to feel loved, receiving the opposite is especially devastating. Negativity can cause wounds so deep that it takes up to ten positive statements to repair the damage of one thoughtless put-down.

"If you can't say something nice, don't say anything at all" is not really a practical strategy. Sometimes you have to talk about unpleasant things and even verbalize negative feelings, but it's helpful to agree on some rules about the kind of words you will use when you talk to one another. Determine what kinds of statements tend to wound each other—you probably already know what they are!—and make those statements off-limits, especially during fights. (It's best to do this together, but even a one-sided decision to avoid negativity can make a significant difference.) As a general rule of thumb, we recommend taking all profanity and name-calling off the table when talking to each other. It's also important to make a habit of *positive* communication—not empty flattery, but honest praise and encouragement—to balance the necessary negatives.

Blaming. From the story of Adam and Eve right up to the headlines of the twenty-first century, you can read about people who habitually blame someone else for their problems. Instead of taking responsibility for our actions, we tend to blame the one closest to us—usually our spouse. But blame is almost never a useful or helpful response to a problem. Maybe your husband was at fault today, but yesterday the fault might have been yours—and you may be equally responsible for many of your problems. We all blow it at times, and none of us likes someone throwing our mistakes in our face. One of the keys to good communication is seeking solutions, not scapegoats. When you choose not to play the blaming game, both of you are freed to move forward.

One of the most helpful ways we know to break the habit of blaming in conversation is the old ploy of using "I" language. When addressing a problem, push yourself to state the problem in terms of how "I" feel about it instead of what "you" (your husband) did. (Instead of "You left the lights on again," you might say, "I would appreciate it if you turned them off when you leave a room.") Yes, it's a gimmick, but we find it helpful because it causes you to be aware of a tendency to focus on blame instead of solutions.

Overload. When my (Alice) husband saw the quote that opens this chapter, he chuckled and said, "How true." Although there are exceptions, women are more likely than men to have a problem with overtalking, especially in relational situations. This is primarily due to differences in the way men and women use language. Women often use talking as a way to connect with others and also as a way of processing their thoughts—they tend to "think out loud," whereas men tend to do their thinking silently and then speak the results out loud. Women are also likely to use many more words than men do in the context of a relationship. As a result, they may leave little room for their husbands, who process ideas differently, to respond. Without even realizing it, they can force their husbands into silence. I (Steve) once saw a bumper sticker that put it this way:

I CAN'T GET A WORD IN EDGEWISE!

When a man is silent, it is easy for his wife to feel like he doesn't care, but maybe the problem is that he is overloaded with too many words and too many details—or he may be trying to formulate a response. Try stopping every three or four sentences to ask for your husband's feedback. Ask for his ideas before you bombard him with the way you have everything figured out. And when you ask, be sure to listen!

151

There's another issue here that may have a simpler solution than you expect. For many women, talking is an important emotional outlet—plus it's fun!—and it's possible you need more of it than your husband can comfortably supply. This doesn't necessarily mean your marriage is deficient. It may mean you just need to spend more time with your girlfriends. Remember, it's not reasonable to expect your husband to meet all your needs. This includes your need for lots of words!

Exaggeration. Exaggeration is a soft word for lying, and many of us are guilty of it every day. We stretch the truth so we look better, get more sympathy, make our point more effectively, or cause a situation to sound more dramatic than it really is.

When talking with your husband, you might exaggerate by using words like *always* and *never:* "You are *never* home on time." "You *never* appreciate what I do." "You *always* yell at the kids." "You are *always* insensitive and rude." If you use this kind of exaggeration, your husband will probably think of an exception, put up his defenses, and the conversation will come to a standstill. Or he'll think, *She doesn't ever notice the times I do things right, so why even try?* Because of this tendency, we believe it's a good rule to banish *always* and *never* from your relationship conversations. It's just an easy way to cut down on the level of defensiveness in your conversations.

Not listening. If being heard and understood is like the fragrance of a rose, then being ignored is like its thorn.

Many arguments are caused by a failure to listen or by selective listening. Really listening to someone means that you stop what you are doing and focus on the other person. You tune in to the feelings behind his words. You involve your face and body language in a welcoming way and clarify by asking questions. Sometimes simply saying, "Tell me more," will open the door to some of the most intimate conversation you have had in a long time.

Dr. Charles Sell writes, "It takes two good listeners to make one good marriage."[6] When two people listen to each other with understanding hearts, it is a sacred gift. And there is a lot you can do for your marriage by improving your listening skills. But what if you, like Kari at the beginning of this chapter, are feeling miffed because you believe your husband doesn't listen to you?

153

Checking your communication for any of the above pitfalls can certainly help; you can actually improve your husband's listening by making yourself easier to listen to. It's also a good idea to ask whether you are being direct enough in what you say (see chapter 3). If the habit of not listening is entrenched, however, you may need to adopt a different strategy. Some women have had good success with sending cards, writing notes on their husbands' calendars, corresponding through e-mail, or speaking on cell phones. And professional counseling can be especially helpful in situations where husbands and wives have lost their ability to listen to one another.

Fighting Fair

Every couple has disagreements—and almost every couple fights from time to time. When you are frustrated and disappointed about your marriage, however, disagreements can easily escalate out of control and cut off all meaningful communication. Fuses are shorter, and tension builds quickly over pressure points like money, sex, household chores, parenting, friends, and other family members. Tempers flare, and your words and actions in the heat of the moment can do further damage to an already faltering relationship.

What's the alternative? Since avoiding disagreement is almost impossible, it's important to negotiate your differences and handle your anger in a way that minimizes damage and even promotes understanding. Rather than avoiding fights, you need to learn to fight fair. Learning how to fight fair will keep you from denying, stuffing, or storing up your anger. Anger that is not expressed in a healthy way easily leads to a breakdown in communication and eventually closes your heart toward your husband.

In my book *20 Surprisingly Simple Rules and Tools for a Great Marriage*, I (Steve) spell out seven practical rules for keeping your fights fair and even productive.[7]

1. *Choose the right time and place.* Most fights occur when one or both of you is very tired, very hungry, or very stressed. If this is true for either of you, we suggest that you simply refuse to engage at that time. If necessary, leave the room. But before you do, make arrangements for a future engagement—and be sure to keep your word. Otherwise,

the situation will never be resolved, and you or your husband may feel abandoned or disrespected.

No matter what, we urge you not to fight in front of your children. They need to see their parents in a healthy relationship, and it is unfair to drag them into your difficulties.

2. *Show respect.* Make it your goal to attack the problem, not the person. Choose your words carefully and avoid belittling your spouse or calling him names. And try to keep the volume down. Yelling can be intimidating, and once it starts, a fight can easily escalate out of control.

3. *Deal with one issue at a time.* In the midst of an argument, it's easy to get off track, and soon you are skipping from one issue to another without resolving anything. Commit to staying on the original issue until it is resolved.

4. *Stay in the present.* When you start focusing on what happened a month or even a day ago, the situation quickly gets complicated. The more time has elapsed from a disputed event, the more chance for distortion or reinventing history. Try your best to stick to the present.

5. *Try not to interrupt.* There's nothing more frustrating than trying to explain something and not being allowed to finish. In the heat of the argument, however, the temptation to interrupt each other can be powerful. One way to solve this problem by using the 3 + 3 rule. Flip a coin to see who gets to start. Talk for three minutes with absolutely no interruptions while the other person listens attentively. Then the second person gets equal time. This process can be repeated until there is nothing more to say.

How to Finish a Fight: Three Possible Resolutions

Accommodation: You or your spouse is willing to change.

Acceptance: One of you won't or can't change—so you choose to live with the situation.

Compromise: You are both willing to change.

STEVE STEPHENS[8]

6. *End with some form of resolution.* It's amazing how many couples have ongoing fights about the same problem because there is never any resolution. Sometimes you have to try a short-term resolution to see how it fits. Other times you simply have to resolve to meet again to discuss your issues further. The important thing is to decide on some course of action before you leave the discussion.

7. *Always make up after a fight.* During most fights, things are said or done that are hurtful, so often it is necessary to apologize before you can make up. After every fight, make it a point to do something to reconnect—take a walk together, hold hands, pray—whatever is a meaningful way for you to reaffirm your love.

The Transforming Power of Love

George Eliot's classic novel *Silas Marner* tells the story of a sad, lonely, and angry man whose chief activities are weaving cloth and hoarding money. He lives in solitude and has no friends. He neither listens nor speaks to people unless it is absolutely necessary. When he does speak, his words are cold. He is a miserable person with miserable communication skills. As the years pass by, Silas Marner's life narrows and hardens as his anger grows into bitterness. Then one day he finds a blond-haired baby girl who has been abandoned by her family. He raises little Eppie and, in the process, his heart softens. He learns to communicate and resolve his anger.

The last paragraph of the book shows the wonderful transformation that can happen to anyone willing to seriously work on communication. Eppie turns to Silas and says, "What a pretty home ours is! I think nobody could be happier than we are."

That statement is our deepest prayer for you and your home.

Something to Try

You can choose just one...

- Find a quiet place to ponder these two questions: *What is it like being married to me? What is it like hearing the words I say?* After thoughtful and honest reflection, write out your answers.

- Of the five bad communication habits listed on pages 149–52, which ones are you most likely to use? How does your husband respond when you do?

- As a guideline, review the seven rules for fighting fair on pages 154–6. Sit down with your husband and make up your own fight-fair rules. Post them somewhere where you can refer to them the next time you have an argument.

- Henry David Thoreau once wrote, "The greatest compliment that was ever paid me was when one asked me what I thought, and attended to my answer." Ask God to show you how you can do this for your husband sometime this week.

Chapter 12

Reconnecting

*Love must be learned,
and learned again and again;
there is no end to it.*

KATHERINE ANNE PORTER

almost forgotten, the blintzes drooped in their sour cream as the handsome young couple laughed about the movie they had seen the night before and bantered back and forth about the literature class they were taking. They intimately shared confessions of childhood pranks and giggled about the memories.

By contrast, a quiet elderly couple sat in the booth across from them. The woman's dress was faded, and the man's head was shiny. She chewed her oatmeal slowly. He nibbled at his hard-boiled egg. Neither spoke a word.

How sad not to have anything to say, thought the young woman. *I hope we never become like that.* A few moments later, however, when she bent down to pick something up from the floor, the beautiful young woman noticed that the older couple's free hands were gently entwined. They had been holding hands all the time.

She was humbled by what she had been privileged to witness. The old man's gentle caress of his wife's tired fingers was a simple and profound act of connection.[1]

Nurturing Togetherness

The above true story, adapted from the writings of Daphna Renan, beautifully illustrates the power of connection and togetherness in marriage. If you are thinking of walking away from your marriage, it might be because you have lost that sense of connectedness. It's easy to reach a point in your marriage where your lives are like two parallel railroad tracks, running side by side without ever touching. You live together, but your lives are mentally, emotionally, and spiritually separate. Connecting again may feel impossible—or like too much work. You may even be tempted simply to start over with a new connection—a fresh and exciting relationship.

The problem with that kind of thinking is that what's new doesn't stay fresh and exciting for very long. The dullness of routine will erode any relationship if you allow it; and even the most loving couple can drift apart. But it doesn't have to happen. Just imagine how wonderful your marriage could be if you would invest the same time, money, and enthusiasm into connecting with your husband that you would invest in connecting with someone new.

How do you make contact again after growing apart— or stay connected over the long haul? We believe the key is reestablishing a sense of togetherness—learning to think "we" instead of "you" and "me" and learning to share many different areas of your lives.

As you read through our suggestions for building togetherness, keep in mind that every marriage is unique. Husbands and wives connect in different ways, and a marriage that is strong in several areas but weak in others can still be in pretty good shape. As a rule of thumb, however, the more you share, the more satisfying your relationship will be. We urge you to do what you can to nurture togetherness in your marriage. In the process, we believe you will rediscover the true meaning of two people becoming one.

Henceforth there will be such a oneness between us— that when one weeps the other will taste salt.

AUTHOR UNKNOWN

Emotional togetherness. A husband and wife who are emotionally connected are aware of and interested in each other's joys, fears, hurts, and frustrations. They know each other's emotional histories and how to read each other's feelings. As they laugh and cry together, they enjoy the amazing gift of multiplying their joys and dividing their sorrows.

Don't be surprised if your husband struggles with emotional togetherness. Women tend to be more comfortable in this area. But women as well as men can be emotionally skittish, and both men and women can learn to connect more effectively in this area.

The key to establishing—or maintaining—this kind of closeness in a marriage is establishing a climate of emotional safety. Each partner must take each other's feelings seriously and avoid the dangers of denying, belittling, or moralizing emotions. In other words, let your feelings bring you closer instead of driving each other apart.

If you've hurt each other in the past, emotional closeness might be the hardest connection to reestablish. Being vulnerable with someone who has betrayed your trust takes courage—and will probably take time. Many couples have found that improving connection in other areas of relationship increases emotional closeness as well.

Intellectual togetherness. This happens when you share ideas and opinions with each other and enjoy "a meeting of the minds." You don't have to agree, but you do have to talk and listen respectfully. It also helps if you make a commitment to explore the world together, engaging your minds as you look into some new topics that one or both of you is curious about. It might help to change your television habits and watch programs on the Discovery Channel or Biography Channel—or get two copies of a book and discuss it. Some couples enjoy taking classes together or attending a couples' Bible study. If you want a real bonus for building intellectual togetherness, find a topic you are both interested in, and research it at the library or on the Internet. The next time you are out to dinner, have fun discussing what you learned.

Practical togetherness. This kind of closeness develops when you tackle the everyday tasks of life together instead of separately. Whether balancing your finances, caring for your children, or doing dozens of household chores, you build camaraderie when you work as a team to accomplish a shared goal. How you do this depends on you. You can accomplish some chores more quickly and easily if you do them side by side. On others, you might prefer to work separately but parcel out the work so you both finish about the same time and can relax together.

If you and your husband are accustomed to working separately on most tasks, we suggest you begin a dialogue about practical togetherness by asking your husband if there are areas where you can help him—and being prepared with some ideas about how he could help you. Another idea would be to pick a project you've been hoping to tackle around the house—something apart from your regular "his" and "hers" tasks—and invite him to work on it with you. Write down a plan for what you hope to accomplish, and see how it goes for a week or so. The plan may have to be revised, and if it does, revise it together.

Practical togetherness doesn't necessarily mean doing *everything* together. Each of you may have tasks you prefer to do alone because you find the work soothing or relaxing, and the logistics of collaborating on certain tasks may be too tricky. That's okay, but keep your eye out for practical activities you can share. And remember, men aren't good at reading your mind, so if you want help with a particular item, *ask*.

Aesthetic togetherness. Seeking, absorbing, and celebrating all that is lovely in life can't help but bring the two of

163

you closer—and the act of enjoying beauty together builds a wonderful archive of shared memories. Not everyone enjoys the same type of beauty, of course. Some are drawn to music, paintings, sculpture, dance, or drama. Others prefer the sights and sounds of creation. The key to building aesthetic togetherness is to find some form of beauty you and your spouse both appreciate—and make a point of sharing it. When you see a spectacular sunset gathering on the horizon or hear a romantic song beginning on the radio, call your husband and ask him if he has a few minutes to share something nice with you. Holding hands while watching the changing colors of a sunset sky or enjoying the interplay of the lyrics and melody can help bind your souls together.

If you want to take another step toward aesthetic togetherness, stretch yourself a little. Make an honest effort to develop an appreciation for a form of beauty your husband likes. Ask him to explain to you why he is drawn to a certain kind of song or landscape and try to see it through his eyes. Ask him to give your idea of beauty a chance too. You may always have areas where you agree to disagree, but even the act of sharing your tastes with one another can bring you a little closer together.

Recreational togetherness. Can a marriage break up for lack of fun? Absolutely! Without a sense of shared playfulness and enjoyment, a relationship can become dull and heavy, and the responsibilities of marriage can seem too much without some form of recreation to lighten things up.

The truth is, the more time you spend playing together, the better you are bound to feel about your relationship. Good, wholesome laughter is a wonderful stress reliever, and *shared* laughter connects you with a pleasant bond. If you want to strengthen the connection between you, we suggest you make playfulness a priority, whether it's reading the comics together, having a tickling contest, watching a funny movie, or playing Ping-Pong. Look for activities you both enjoy, and make time to enjoy them together.

Keep in mind that the activities you share don't always have to be your absolute favorite pastimes. When you were dating, you probably enjoyed a lot of fun things just for the purpose of being together. Maybe you joined him on the couch to watch basketball or got up early to go fishing with him—or he took you to a romantic movie and ate quiche with you at a sidewalk café. Once your marriage was established, however, you may have fallen into a pattern of pursuing your separate interests. And this is not an awful thing—as long as you maintain some activities you enjoying doing together as well.

To combat this "play separately" tendency, Dr. Willard F. Harley suggests the following exercise: You and your husband should each make a list of all the activities you enjoy—the longer the lists, the better. Write down everything you can think of, from hiking to coin collecting. Combine the two lists, listing everything alphabetically. Then each of you rate every activity on a scale from minus 4 (absolutely hate) to plus 4 (absolutely love). Eliminate any item to which you *both* do not assign a positive score, and what's left will be interests you *both* enjoy to some degree. They're the ones to focus on as you work on building recreational togetherness.[2]

Social togetherness. Even if one or both of you is not the "social type," we urge you to look for opportunities to spend time with people and groups you both enjoy (even a little). Family gatherings, church events, and evenings with friends can strengthen your marriage by building a sense of how you as a couple fit into the larger community—as well as establishing a support network to lift you up during the hard times.

Because other people can make or break your marriage, however, it pays to be careful to choose your social contacts wisely. Seek out godly friends, wise colleagues, and maybe even a mentoring couple who can help you celebrate the good times and survive the tough times. In particular, look for mutual friends who are committed to their own marriages and who will help you hold it together when things get difficult.

Sexual togetherness. If your relationship with your husband has grown so distant that you are thinking of leaving, you may be annoyed or angry that we would even write about sexual togetherness. But we must because we believe God created sex as the glue that binds a man and woman together. It is also a gift you give each other to prove your commitment. Giving your bodies to each other symbolizes the giving of your hearts.

If you no longer enjoy making love with your husband—or if he has withdrawn that gift from you—pray that the Lord will rekindle your desire. Pray that your husband will become more tender, considerate, and romantic. It's not a bad idea to consult your family physician as well, because certain physical conditions can affect the level of desire in a marriage.

A Connecting Conversation

Ask each other the following questions...

- ❧ What is the difference between having sex and making love?

- ❧ Is there anything about our intimate life that could be improved upon?

- ❧ How can we better connect heart-to-heart?

- ❧ What are your dreams for the future?

- ❧ Do we regularly connect soul-to-soul?

- ❧ How could we make connecting soul-to-soul a priority?

- ❧ Is there anything I need to seek your forgiveness for?

- ❧ What do you love most about our marriage?

LYSA TERKEURST[3]

As you grow closer in other areas of your marriage, you may well find that your sexual relationship warms up as well. In the book *Capture His Heart,* Lysa TerKeurst suggests some more specific ways to add some heat:

To truly get to know your husband and for him to truly know you, you will have to spend time communicating and exploring this awesome gift from God together. Guide your husband's hands to touch you where it brings you pleasure. Show him how to be tender in some places and aggressive in others as he caresses you and holds you. Tell him where you enjoy his kisses. The more you communicate and open yourself up to your husband, the more he can understand how to truly satisfy you and the more satisfied he will be as well.[4]

Spiritual togetherness. God never intended that a couple face the joys and sorrows of life without Him. He wants to be your ultimate strength and refuge during the best and hardest years together. When a couple looks beyond themselves and builds an intimate relationship with God, it's amazing what happens in their marriage. Disappointments become easier to tolerate, overwhelming problems easier to handle. Perhaps more than any other "connection," the one where God is the center is the most sustaining part of your marriage.

If you have kept the covenant you made at the beginning of this book and have been praying for your husband fifteen minutes a day, you have already made a start in nurturing spiritual togetherness. The next step is to let your husband know you are praying for him. Before you go your separate ways in the morning, ask your husband how you can pray for him that day. Perhaps he has a stressful task at work or a difficult appointment, or maybe he is just weary from the strenuous demands of his job. Maybe he in turn will ask how he can pray for you, but even if he doesn't, make his requests part of your prayer vigil for him. At night, make it a habit to kneel at your bedside and thank the Lord for one positive thing about your husband. If he is willing, ask your husband to kneel with you so you can pray for one another out loud or silently.

Caring Days

No matter how separate you have become in your marriage, we believe you can become a "we" again. Perhaps you can put a marker in this chapter and daily focus on one of the eight categories of togetherness. You may be surprised at how many problems you can solve once you become more connected with your husband. In the meantime, here is an exercise that can help you jump-start the reconnecting process.[5]

At the top of two separate sheets of paper, write the words "I feel loved when…" and, down the side, write the numbers one through ten. You complete one paper and ask your husband to complete the other. You can write things like, "Call me when you will be more than fifteen minutes late," "Pick up your dirty clothes and put them in the hamper," "Kiss me when you come home," or "Hold my hand when we pray." Whatever will make you feel loved, write it down. Your husband might write down items like, "Give me a five-minute back rub" or "Let me watch *Monday Night Football* without complaining."

When you are through, trade lists—no fair criticizing what the other person writes! Then try to do one thing on your spouse's list every day. (If you're a worn-out woman, doing one item each week might be more realistic.) Determine to make every day a caring day, and watch how the Lord will draw the two of you together—one man, one woman, one flesh, one life.

Something to Try

You can choose just one...

- Grade your marriage (A, B, C, D, or F) in each of the eight areas of togetherness:

  ____ Emotional   ____ Intellectual

  ____ Practical   ____ Aesthetic

  ____ Recreational   ____ Social

  ____ Sexual   ____ Spiritual

  Spend some time talking to your husband about any areas that you have graded A or B. Make sure he knows how much you appreciate what he does to help your relationship make such high grades in these areas.

- Choose one segment of togetherness that has a low grade, and discuss it with your husband. (He may grade it differently than you do!) Brainstorm together to come up with a plan to improve. Take the first steps to implement the plan before the week is over.

- Complete the exercise at the end of this chapter in which you and your husband each write down ten items to complete the statement, "I feel loved when...." Get two empty jars and write your name on one and his name on the other. Cut the lists of ten ideas into strips, and put them in the jars. Each day (or once a week), each of you pick from the other's jar one activity to do. Keep it a secret, but make sure to commit to doing for each other what the slip of paper you've chosen says.[6]

Chapter 13

Take Care of Yourself

I love people. I love my family, my children.
But inside myself is a place
where I live all alone and that's where
you renew your springs that never dry up.

PEARL S. BUCK

robin is the kind of woman who lights up a room when she walks in. People smile when they meet her for the first time, and they keep smiling when they think of her later. But until recently, Robin's family had an entirely different image of her. In her more private world, Robin was often impatient, short-tempered, and moody. She was negative toward her husband and angry with her kids. She didn't want to be that way, but home was the only place where she felt safe enough to show how exhausted and out of control she really was. Robin felt overwhelmed, stressed, and ready to do almost anything to escape the never-ending drain of feeling worn out.

As long as people didn't get too close, Robin looked winsome and energetic. At home she was a worn-out woman. This was her little secret—a secret that threatened to tear apart her marriage, her family, and her life.

Overwhelmed and Worn Out

When we were doing research for our previous book, *The Worn Out Woman,* we were amazed to discover just how weary the average American woman is. Recent studies show that more than 60 million women in the United States consider themselves overwhelmed. Another 60 million say they are on the fast track to exhaustion. When a woman's energy is depleted, the drain affects her marriage, children, career, friendships, and intimacy with God. It's not a big leap to conclude that being a worn-out woman might set you up for becoming a walk-out woman. When you are weary, it can be tempting to give up on your marriage—especially when you're convinced your husband is the one who is wearing you out.

174

Most books, seminars, and talk shows on marriage stress that successful marriages don't *just happen.* Good marriages require a lot of time and energy. Wonderful marriages require even more. But when you are worn out physically, emotionally, and spiritually, you just don't have time or energy to give. What's more, you probably don't *want* to give them. You want a break—something that will take the pressure off and give you a breath of fresh air. You might even be tempted to look for something new and exciting that will lift you out of the doldrums, at least for a while.

Empty Vessels

In the soul of every weary woman is a deep longing—an almost hurtful ache—to be cared for and nurtured. It's almost like wanting to be wrapped in a soft comforter, held in loving arms, and gently rocked. But the very nature of being a wife and perhaps a mother makes it difficult for most women to find that kind of nurture—or even admit she needs it. Instead, she is expected to dole out care and comfort to others. But the hard truth is that it's hard to pour from an empty vessel. A worn-out woman has very little to give.

What's the solution to this worn-out dilemma? The complete answer can fill an entire book or more—and we do just that in *The Worn Out Woman*. But the short answer is that a worn-out woman cannot expect to receive the nurture she craves unless she recognizes her need, accepts it, and takes steps to see that her most important needs are met.

We're not saying the key to energizing the worn-out woman is for the husband to do more—although he must be part of solution. We've found that most exhausted women are depleted because of their own decisions to do too much and to shortchange their own needs. The first step in reducing the worn-out cycle, therefore, is facing your own responsibility to take care of yourself and see that your basic needs are met.

In order to function over the long term, to keep your relationships healthy, and to live as the person God had in mind for you to be, we believe you need:

∞ An active relationship with God to keep your connection with the source of all comfort.

∞ Adequate physical rest to allow your brain to process events and your body to replenish your energy reserves.

∞ Enough exercise to help you handle stress and keep your body strong, energetic, and flexible.

∞ Regular, healthy meals to provide energy, to regulate blood sugar and hormone levels, and to break up your day.

∞ Time for yourself to develop inner resources which will reenergize and bring comfort to your body, mind, and spirit.

∞ A caring support system to provide you with love, encouragement, and affirmation.

Accept life daily not as a cup to be drained but as a chalice to be filled with whatsoever things are honest, pure, lovely, and of good report.

AUTHOR UNKNOWN

Keep in mind that all of these are real needs, not self-indulgent luxuries. Learning healthy ways to get them met accomplishes far more than just a temporary lift out of the doldrums. It has the power to reenergize all areas of your life, including your marriage. Your husband needs you to take care of yourself. If you don't, you may develop physical problems that hinder your ability to care for your family. Psychological problems such as depression or anxiety are likely too. At the very least, you will probably grow angry and resentful, and those feelings in themselves have the power to turn a marriage that was once so sweet into something that is pungent and sour.

In our hurry-up-gotta-get-it-done culture, some people might confuse self-nurture with self-indulgence. But we are not recommending that you abandon your husband and children and spend your days lounging at the spa. We believe that taking care of yourself is a responsibility too. It's an act of stewardship, of caring for the life God gave us. It's also a way of avoiding burnout and seeing that you have the vitality you need to nurture your most sacred relationships—including your marriage. Here are just a few tactics that can help you care for yourself to replenish your life:

Ask for help. If necessary, *cry* for help—and make your first cry to the Lord. Remember that He made you, needs and all—and He cares for you deeply. In the Bible, the prophet Isaiah describes God's loving concern this way: "He tends his flock like a shepherd: He gathers the lambs in his arms and carries them close to his heart."[1] When it comes to taking care of yourself, soul nurturing is where your empty well begins to fill. Every minute you spend with God in prayer or meditation, every verse you read and reread from the Bible, every hymn you sing to yourself as you drive to the next errand can strengthen you and keep you going.

In addition to leaning on the Lord, we urge you to seek the wise counsel of a trusted friend or a counselor. If your marriage is shaky, you might consider doing this even before you talk to your husband about your need for help. You need someone who will share your burden and also hold you accountable for making the necessary changes in your life to care for yourself.

Involve your family to negotiate a plan. If you have deferred taking care of yourself for a while, your family has probably grown accustomed to that arrangement. They think it's normal, and they may not realize how overwhelmed you're feeling. The only way to change your situation is to raise an alarm. We urge you to talk seriously with your husband about your needs and why they are so important. Do this without blaming, and don't be surprised if his initial response is a bit defensive. Just take a deep breath and calmly explain how exhausted or lonely you feel. Share with him what you have tried to do to make things better—describing what has worked and what hasn't. Let him know that feeling worn out blocks you from being the sort of loving, caring, exciting wife you want to be.

After you have explained the problem to your husband, ask for his ideas and his help in making a plan to reduce your stress. It's probably helpful to give him the option of processing for a few days before you decide together on a specific plan for the whole family. This could involve anything from a family chore day to a different child-care arrangement to a quarterly getaway with or without friends at a local retreat center.

Once you've come up with a plan, give it a week or two (no more), and then talk again and evaluate whether or not it's working. Changing the way your family operates can be challenging for both you and your family. It may take several tries—and you may find that you must give up control of certain areas to get the relief you need. But we believe you'll find the payoff of increased energy, reduced stress, and healthier relationships is worth the effort.

Put self-care on your calendar. One of the biggest challenges of self-care is finding the time—when there just isn't any extra time to find. We doubt you will suddenly discover a blank spot on your schedule where you can pencil in a nap or a workout or even a bubble bath. But that's just the point. In order to have time for self-care, you need to *put* it on your schedule. Write in appointments for putting your feet up and relaxing while you do something you really enjoy. And don't just pencil them in—write them in ink, as a commitment.

Even though I (Steve) know it's important to take Tami out for special afternoon or evening dates, my best intentions can easily get crowded out of my schedule. I love it when Tami takes my calendar and writes in an "appointment" for us. If it's written down, it somehow has more priority and is more likely to happen. And I appreciate the fact that my wife cares enough about our marriage and her own needs to do this.

Practice saying yes selectively. It's always been hard for me (Alice) to pace myself. Starting when I was a freshman in high school, I was often too busy *doing* to pay attention to *being* the woman God wanted me to be. As a young wife and mother, I would sometimes be so exhausted that I wanted to curl up and sleep the week away, but the adrenaline rush of a packed schedule and last-minute deadlines kept me going. In fact, my life was so busy I hardly noticed the toll my busyness was taking on my family. Perhaps it's because I'm now in the season of life called "older and wiser" (and yes, less energy), but I'm finally learning to say yes more selectively—and to say no when I have to.

If you are a woman who loves "to do," then prioritizing your yeses is one way to reserve time to take care of yourself. For instance, before saying yes to another project or agreeing to work more hours at the office, try to delay your answer until you have answered the following questions:

- How will this activity affect my family?

- How will I feel about my decision in two weeks?

- What is my motivation for saying yes?

- Has God equipped me to do this?

- Will saying yes make God smile?

- Can I take on this new task and still have time to be the person God wants me to be?

Remember that if you always say yes, people will keep asking for more—and "more" can have deadly consequences for you and your marriage. Your time and your energy are limited, so try to save your yeses for the people and things that really matter to you.

Adjust your plan for the seasons of your life. There are seasons of a woman's life when relaxation advice seems like a tasteless joke. If you have toddlers or a large family, that's probably how you feel right now. Even if your children are older, you might feel it's impossible to relax when you are juggling a career, ministry, social life, home, marriage, and caring for older parents. In the course of your lifetime, you will move in and out of seasons when you feel like you're trying to hold ten Ping-Pong balls under water with one hand tied behind your back. Even when you think you have everything under control, something else pops up.

What do you do during busy seasons like these? It may really help to remind yourself that they *are* seasons—that children grow, circumstances change, and many tasks grow easier with time. It also helps to focus on the blessings that busy seasons can bring and do your best to enjoy them. (Your babies will only be babies for a short time.) But you still need to do what you can to take care of yourself—so your busy times don't do you in! In fact, it's in those seasons when you can't find the time to relax that you may need it the most.

If you have young children and do not have to work full time outside your home, one way to take care of yourself is to find out about MOPS (Mothers of Preschoolers) or similar organizations. These provide fun activities that keep children occupied while moms interact with *adults*. There is something quite refreshing about spending upbeat time with a group of women—especially when someone else is providing good care for the little ones. Another idea is to exchange child care once or twice a week with another mom and to use these times for simple pleasures (see next page).

Cultivate small changes and simple pleasures. Even during those times where responsibilities are heavy and time is short, you can do wonders for your spirit by learning to take "mini breaks" to enjoy simple pleasures. Five minutes of stretching and deep breathing, ten minutes for a cup of tea, fifteen minutes for prayer and meditation, or a walk around the block in the sunshine can do wonders for your body, mind, and spirit. Even if you are home full-time with small children, you can often carve out little moments. Claim them! In a rare moment when everyone is down for a nap, take a bubble bath instead of starting another load of laundry. Or put on a CD you love, and invite everyone in the house to join you in a dance.

Reduce your stress by journaling. When problems exist, it is easy to fall into a downward spiral of negative thinking about yourself, your children, life in general, and especially about your husband. Some level of depression comes creeping in and along with it an overwhelming sense of tiredness and a need to withdraw. Sometimes it seems like a heavy gray blanket is blocking the view of anything good. It may surprise you to learn that keeping a journal can pull you out of that spiral. Recent research, in fact, shows that 70 percent of people experiencing these moods can be turned around by the simple act of journaling.

There's nothing mysterious about keeping a journal, and there are no rules. All you really need is a notebook of some kind—even a school-type spiral will do—and something to write with. You can write every day, diary style, or you can pick up your journal when the spirit moves. The point is to get your thoughts and emotions on paper instead of letting them ricochet around in your head.

Three Simple Pleasures

1.

Look through old photos with no goal of organizing them.
Just enjoy them and relive the memories.

2.

Read some chapters in a book you've wanted to read.
Determine at the outset how many chapters
you are going to read,
and then do it in total freedom.

3.

Spend some energy in a leisurely atmosphere
with no other agenda.
Go bowling, roller-skate, hike, jump rope,
dance through the house.
Fly a kite, shoot some baskets, ride a bike.

KIM THOMAS[2]

Some people find it helpful to set aside sections of their journals for specific kinds of thoughts. In a section labeled "gratitude," you could try to write down at least two or three items daily for which you are thankful. Seeing your list grow over time will actually stoke your sense of gratitude. Another section of your journal might be called feelings. It's okay to write when you're brutally angry as well as when you are unbelievably happy. When you look back over a period of time, you will probably be amazed at how much your feelings fluctuate, and you'll realize anew how important it is to make decisions based on wisdom and reason—not just emotion. Still another section of your journal can be dedicated to problem solving. Here's where you write lists of the pros and cons to help you clarify issues and make better choices.

184

You don't have to organize your journal this way, of course. It's your journal, and you may write in it any way that feels comfortable and fits with your unique personality. You can just scribble spontaneously or randomly, if that's more your style. If you journal in the morning, try focusing on what you are looking forward to during the day or what needs to be resolved from the day before. At bedtime, try to ramp down your emotions by writing thoughts of gratitude and love letters to God. Whenever you do it, the process of writing will help lift that gray-blanket feeling and allow good things to come back into view. If you are not currently journaling on a regular basis, we encourage you to try writing *something* every day for at least a month, even if it's just one or two sentences.

Robin's Private World

For Robin, the woman we talked about at the beginning of this chapter, journaling was one of the ways she started paying attention to what her worn-out life was saying to her. More importantly, journaling quieted her heart enough to let her hear what God was saying to her. Beginning a journal was just one of the dramatic and positive developments in Robin's life that have changed her from a worn-out (and potential walk-out) woman to a happy, productive, and fulfilled wife and mother.

Finding a mentor was another positive step for Robin. She had always admired the serenity and wisdom of one particular woman at church. After a serious blowup with her family, Robin decided to call that woman for help. Looking back at that first meeting, Robin says, "Most of the time I just cried. In between long, deep, inconsolable sobs, I choked out short little sentences. 'If Dan would try harder to be more sensitive and encouraging, I wouldn't feel this way.' 'If the kids were more helpful, then I wouldn't have to get so angry.' It was probably more than an hour before I finally admitted that some of what was happening was my fault. In my attempt to make everyone happy and live up to impossible expectations, I had taken on more commitments than I could handle. It was really hard, but just saying all this out loud to that dear lady, who kept holding my hand, somehow made me feel better."

With the help of her new friend, Robin sorted out which commitments she could reasonably finish and which ones she needed to let go. When Robin contacted the people involved and explained that she had taken on too much and asked to be released from some of her responsibilities, she was surprised at how understanding and gracious everyone was. It took several months, but Robin gradually started feeling restored and refreshed. This sentence from her journal sums up the difference in her life: "I feel like every day is sprinkled with sunshine."

More than two years later, Robin is still practicing what she learned during that time of family crisis. Instead of saying yes to most every request like she used to do, Robin purposely evaluates each one. She asks herself hard questions like the ones listed on page 180. Then, after Robin considers her answers, she sits down with her husband, Dan, and asks for his input. As it turns out, this additional step has had a very positive effect on their marriage. In the beginning, Dan shrugged it off and told her to do whatever she thought was best. But when Robin convinced him that she really wanted and needed his advice, Dan felt honored and took seriously his role of adviser and protector.

Life has changed significantly for Robin. She feels great about the progress she's made toward taking care of herself. Along with spiritual nurturing and exercise, she has found some new interests (scrapbooking and golf, which she and Dan enjoy doing together).

Robin still lights up the room when she walks in, and people still keep smiling when they think about her. The main difference is that when Robin is in her private world of home and family, the smiles continue. Because she is caring for herself, she also has energy and vitality for the people she loves the most.

Something to Try

You can choose just one...

- Write down five things that are both relaxing and pleasurable for you. Make the time to do at least one of these sometime this week, even if it means delaying something else. Schedule your nurturing time on your calendar, and highlight it in yellow.

- Betty Ackerman of Offerie, Kansas, says, "In my family we each have a night assigned to do the dinner dishes. On Saturdays we each pick a room to clean."[3] Gather your family together and discuss implementing this idea or something similar to distribute your family workload a little more equitably.

- If you don't already have a journal, stop at a bookstore and browse in the journal section. Notice the various designs, the texture of the pages, whether or not there is a ribbon bookmark, and whether the pages are lined or unlined. Buy something lovely that you will enjoy using.

- Pick a small bouquet of wildflowers, or stop by a florist and select a few daisies or tea roses. Put them in a small glass jar, and color the water with food coloring. Place them on your desk or by the kitchen sink as a reminder to take care of yourself.

Chapter 14

The Fantasy of Something Better

*If you're going to fantasize and daydream,
fantasize and daydream about each other.*

THOMAS KINKADE[1]

oday my (Alice's) heart is aching for my friend Amy. A few weeks ago she moved out of her home—away from her family—and into a nearby apartment. During our last conversation, Amy insisted she wasn't involved with another man in "that way" but admitted there is a guy who is "a friend." They only meet once a week—just to talk. Even so, I begged her to think about the danger of sharing with him on an intimate emotional level, because sharing your heart can easily lead to sharing your body. Amy is sure this won't happen to her. She just needs time to think things over, she told me. That's why she moved out.

Amy is convinced that what she says is true—at least for the moment. But my heart aches for her because I fear she is fooling herself.

Many women at some point in their marriage think about walking away and getting a new start. Some ponder the idea for years, while for others the thought comes and goes as quickly as the sunset. But what we find startling is the number of women who are currently acting on the thought. These are smart women, good mothers, trustworthy friends, committed Christians, hardworking employees, respected neighbors, compassionate people—women of every age and type.

Perhaps it's because of the mounting stress of living in the twenty-first century. Certainly the rise in physical, emotional, and chemical abuse is a factor. Add sliding morals and our "throwaway mentality" into the mix, stir in disappointment and discontent, and breaking the marriage vows can seem understandable and almost justifiable. It can *look* like the best option in a bad situation.

The trouble, of course, is that it's not.

The idea that you can just start over and get everything right when everything went wrong before is simply a fantasy—and a dangerous fallacy as well.

Are You Vulnerable?

It is extremely important that you do not misunderstand our intent in this chapter. We are *not* saying that every woman who is thinking of leaving her husband is involved in an affair—or is even interested in one. In fact, most of the women we talked to in the process of writing this book told us they had no interest in getting romantically involved with another man. But we have come to believe that women in unfulfilling marriages are especially vulnerable to affairs because they often underestimate their own unhappiness. Although they might not intentionally seek other male companionship, a brief encounter or casual comment with someone who is kind and considerate can trigger a rush of longings. It is at this point that the marriage is in real danger. One woman who was thinking of leaving her marriage told us: "It was friendship with another man along with my husband's consistent neglect and disrespect of me that was the trigger."

None of the women I (Alice) have talked to who became involved in affairs actually planned for them to happen. The common factor with these women is that someone they knew as a friend began to connect with them emotionally. Perhaps it was a coworker, a neighbor, or a person they knew at church. Often the attraction started with something small like a compliment, a casual lunch together at work, or even a lingering look.

Keep in mind that it's possible to give in to the "I can do better" fantasy without actually becoming sexually involved. Dave Carder, coauthor of *Torn Asunder: Recovering from Extramarital Affairs,* says this about emotional affairs:

An emotional affair without sex occurs when two parties share their feelings for each other. These affairs are supercharged with emotion. The sound of her voice, the style of his e-mail—they are all loaded. But if you confront them, they'll insist they've done nothing wrong. These secret emotional affairs are powerful influences in the individuals' lives. They often live in a fantasy world, where they imagine what the other party is doing.[2]

In my practice, I (Steve) see a trend that alarms me—a relatively new version of this illusion. Increasingly, I meet women who are living out their fantasies on the Internet. "It's just a game," said one of my clients. "I don't know the men and they don't know me, so how can it be wrong?" Women who think an Internet affair is safe and innocent couldn't be more wrong. Like quicksand, it keeps sucking you in deeper and deeper even when you are seriously trying to get out. It progresses quickly from curiosity to flirtation, to emotional involvement, and eventually to contact. Even if you resist actually meeting a man, once you start sharing on an emotional level, this fantasy person has captured part of your heart and soon will seem better and more interesting than your husband.

Why Fantasies Can Hurt You

Whether acted out on the Net or in real life, such fantasies can be harmful for a number of important reasons—aside from the difficulties of divorce we talked about in chapter 6. The most obvious is that even an emotional affair can cause irreparable damage to an imperfect but workable relationship. Nothing hurts like betrayal. And while a marriage can recover from an affair, the road to such recovery can be steep and painful.

Yet another danger of "I can do better" fantasies is that they are usually just that—fantasies. They are usually based on delusions and can lead to even deeper disappointment than what you are now facing. After all, anyone can put on a good front for a short period of time—or in cyberspace. But the handsome, charming, exciting—or gentle, understanding, and tender—man you believe will rescue you from your relational doldrums is likely to look quite different once you really get to know him. If he is single and knows you are married, research shows that he is most likely narcissistic, alcoholic, or has problems with commitment. If he is married as well, then you are getting involved with a married man who cheats on his wife. Is that really the kind of person you believe will help you discover something better?

In *The Many Loves of Marriage,* artist and author Thomas Kinkade points out another important problem with fantasizing about the perfect person or the perfect relationship:

People get a divorce, link up with someone new, and suddenly they're doing all the fun, romantic stuff— moonlight walks and bicycle rides and exotic getaways. They could have done all of those things with the spouse they just left, but they didn't. As a result, they endure the trauma and humiliation of a wrenching divorce, shattering change in their lives, great financial loss, and bitter, deeply wounded children…all for the sake of "new romantic experiences."

And then Kinkade asks a very pertinent question: "And how long do you think *that* relationship will last?"[3]

As men and women have discovered through the ages, infidelity and delusion form a very shaky foundation for happiness. No matter how painful your marriage is now and how unhappy you are in it, your chances of finding lasting happiness in the form of "someone better" are slim indeed. Doesn't it make more sense to invest your time, energy, and emotions into making your current marriage better?

194

Five Fatal Fallacies About Affairs

- It could never happen to me.

- We are only friends.

- If it feels so good, it can't be so bad.

- I can stop anytime I want.

- Nobody is going to get hurt.

ROBERT JEFFRESS[4]

Have You Gone Too Far?

The idea of "I can do better than this" often begins with seemingly innocent questions like "What if I were single?" or "What if I had married someone else?" These questions are reinforced by the idealistic—and unrealistic—depiction of love in romantic movies, television, music, and novels. It's easy to become attached to the illusion of finding someone other than your husband who can meet all your wants, needs, and desires.

Remember that every time you think about being with someone other than your husband, you are undermining your marriage and breaking your vows. God's Word is clear that fantasizing about having sex with anyone other than your spouse is sin.[5] That may sound severe, but every sin that we eventually act out in our bodies begins in our minds—and the easiest place to stop it is in the mind as well.

The first step in ending an affair, in other words, is never allowing it to start. If there is someone you are seriously attracted to—whether a checker at the grocery store, a friend's husband, or someone you met casually—we urge you to do what you must to put him out of your thoughts. In most cases, this will involve avoiding all contact with the person.

One woman found herself very attracted to a man at her church. They had never met, but he was the kind of man women notice, and seeing him stirred her romantic imagination. She changed where she sat in church so he wasn't in her line of vision and avoided places where she might bump into him. Eventually he moved away and she was thankful she had succeeded in never having a conversation with the handsome gentleman.

If you have allowed conversations with another man (whether in person, on the phone, or on the Internet) to move to a personal level, you may be on the brink of or already involved in an emotional affair. Dennis Rainey, award-winning author and the founder of FamilyLife ministries, gives the following seven warning signs that you are too involved:

- ✍ You've got a need you feel your mate isn't meeting— for attention, approval, affection—and that other person begins meeting your need.

- ✍ You find it easier to unwind with someone other than your spouse by dissecting the day's difficulties over lunch, coffee, or during a ride home.

- ✍ You begin to talk about problems you are having with your spouse.

- ✍ You rationalize the relationship by saying that surely it must be God's will to talk so openly and honestly with a fellow Christian. You become defensive about the relationship and protective of it.

- ✍ You look forward to being with this person more than with your own mate.

- You wonder what you'd do if you didn't have this friend to talk to.

- You hide the relationship from your mate.[6]

Another quick test is to ask yourself if you would like your husband to know about or to listen to the conversations you are having. If your answer is no to either question, chances are that you have gone too far.

What should you do if that's the case? We urge you to break off your connection with that individual immediately, no matter how fulfilling your conversations have become. This means no more e-mails, no more meeting for lunch or coffee, no more private conversations. Period. Fill the void by choosing a girlfriend or a mentor who is in a healthy marriage and ask if you can vent with her for a few months while your marriage gets back on track.

If you are involved sexually with someone other than your husband, it's even more crucial that you make a commitment right now to end the affair immediately. Do it today. We suggest you follow the steps listed in the sidebar on the next page.

It is important to follow *all* of the steps, including telling your husband. Secrecy is the dark tunnel through which affairs travel, and the light must be turned on and the tunnel closed. The only exception would be if your husband has a pattern of abuse. If this is true in your situation, then we encourage you to seek the help of a trained counselor who will help you know how much and when to disclose the situation to your husband.

How to End an Affair the Right Way

- *Tell your spouse* about the affair.

- *Make a verbal and written commitment* to your spouse never to see or talk to your lover again.

- *Write a letter* ending the relationship to your lover and send it with the approval of your spouse.

- *Take extraordinary precautions* to guarantee total separation from your lover in the future. If necessary, change your e-mail address, telephone number, cell phone number, and pager numbers. If you are coworkers, a job change or relocation may be needed.

- *Allow your spouse* to monitor voice mail and regular mail for as long as he deems necessary.

- *Both you and your spouse should give each other a twenty-four-hour daily schedule* with locations and telephone numbers to account for your time. Continue this until your spouse feels completely comfortable that you will not cheat again.

- *Make all future financial decisions jointly,* and give each other a complete account of money spent.

- *Commit to spending your leisure time together.*

WILLARD HARLEY JR. AND JENNIFER HARLEY CHALMERS[7]

Telling your husband about an affair doesn't have to mean the end of your marriage. Such disclosure, in fact, often means the beginning of healing and trust. Now is a good time to ask someone to help keep you accountable. Whether it is a pastor, a counselor, or trusted friends, ask them not only to help you get over the affair, but also to help you work on your marriage. For at least a year, you and your husband need to meet together at least once or twice a month with someone you both consider competent, wise, and trustworthy.

Short-Circuiting the "I Can Do Better" Fantasy

To avoid even the temptation of an affair, we invite you to be more selective about what you read and what you watch on television and in the movies. If you enjoy reading romance novels, Christian bookstores and web pages for various Christian publishers will have wholesome recommendations. There are many movies that feature healthy, character-building romances. Watch these together with your husband, and then share with each other what you liked and disliked and how you might use the ideas in your marriage. When it comes to music, stop listening to songs that tear down husbands or glorify affairs. Instead, burn a couple of CDs with love songs that you and your husband both enjoy and play them often.

The most important step you can take to affair-proof your marriage, however, is to improve the connection

between you and your husband. Keeping fun and excitement in your marriage, praying daily for your marriage,
and having close friends who are happily married are some
of your best defenses against temptation. The suggestions
for reconnecting in chapter 12 will give you a good place to
start. We urge you to try one or two on a regular basis—
and watch the changes start to happen.

We're not saying your marriage will become wonderful
overnight. That's fantasy too. Your problems took months
and years to develop. They will probably take months and
years to solve—and some will never be completely fixed in
this life. But if you make the effort to stick it out, we
believe you'll discover a love far more satisfying than your
fantasies could ever provide.

There's really nothing wrong with wanting something
better. In fact, you *should* want something better. But
doesn't it make more sense to seek it in reality rather than
fantasy—working to create something better with the man
you promised to love for a lifetime?

Something to Try

You can choose just one...

- Marriage counselors report that any person given the right circumstances is capable of an affair. What are some of the reasons you think women fall into affairs? What are some of the reasons you think men do? What circumstances would be most likely to cause you (or did cause you) to fall into an affair?

- Have you ever been attracted to someone other than your husband? How did you handle the situation, and how did it affect your marriage?

- Review the warning signs on pages 196–7, and *immediately* change any habits, activities, or relationships that could possibly lure you into an affair.

- There are several resources in the recommended reading list that will help you avoid having an affair or help your marriage survive after an affair is ended. Select one and make a promise to read it all the way through.

Chapter 15

Doesn't God Want Me to Be Happy?

What if God designed marriage to make us holy more than to make us happy?

GARY THOMAS

deep inside we all have a yearning to be happy. We long to skip through sunny meadows holding hands with the one we love or to lie beneath a velvet sky nestled in one another's arms.

We are sincere when we wish others a happy new year, happy anniversary, or happy birthday, and we wish we could achieve happiness for ourselves as easily as blowing out our birthday candles. Even the Declaration of Independence promises the right to pursue happiness as though it could be found merely by chasing a dream. But happiness can be an elusive thing, like the tide. One moment it rushes in and splashes all around us. The next minute we watch it retreat, leaving only wet sand beneath our feet.

Many of the women we have talked to who plan on walking away from their marriages say things like, "I wish things were different, but I'm just not happy anymore. In

203

fact, I haven't been happy for a long time. It's not that I want to hurt my husband, but I can't imagine that God would want me to stay in a marriage where I'm not happy."

When someone who is in a struggling relationship tells us what she means by happiness, she usually begins by describing companionship—shared activities, uplifting conversations, common goals, and exciting adventures. But often, within minutes, there is a significant change as a deep sadness begins to well up in her heart. Her eyes fill with tears as she haltingly describes happiness as being treasured, cared for, protected, and understood.

When you consider the deep longings expressed by these last few words, is it any wonder a woman asks, "Doesn't God want me to be happy?"

Looking in the Wrong Places

Why is happiness so elusive? It's partly because we tend to look for it, like love, in all the wrong places. We interpret God's promise of an abundant life to mean that we can enjoy a heavenlike existence on earth—with no sorrows, no hardships, no tears. We expect all our dreams to be fulfilled here and now, so we look for it in our circumstances, our experiences, our possessions, and yes, in our marriages.

The problem is, these things were never intended to be dependable sources of happiness. As long as we keep expecting these earthly things to make us happy, we are doomed to be disappointed again and again.

In one of the Psalms, King David writes these words to God, *"You* have made known to me the path of life; *you* will fill me with joy in *your* presence, with eternal pleasures at *your* right hand."[1] Note that he doesn't say, "You and my wife," or "You and my children," or "You and my marriage." God gave marriage as a precious gift to a man and a woman, but He never intended it to fulfill all our needs and desires. That is a role God reserved for Himself. He alone can satisfy the deep longings of our souls.

Whether they are husbands, friends, parents, or children, people will eventually disappoint us. Even the best people have times when they are selfish, immature, and forgetful. But God is never this way. His love is the only love that is everlasting and will never fail.[2]

If you are like so many of the women we have talked to, you understand the deep sadness of having a husband who does not seem to cherish you. He has disappointed you over and over again. He might not even realize how much he has hurt you, but his actions have caused wounds so painful that you may have all but lost your feelings of love for him.

Of *course* you are not happy! No one would be happy under circumstances like that.

Marriage is like a freeway and divorce is an off-ramp.
As long as you insist on getting off the freeway,
you never complete the course God has set before you.

AUTHOR UNKNOWN

Happiness from the Source

Dear reader, even though we know your heart is wounded, we are going to ask you a difficult question. We ask because we know you can't depend on your husband or any other person to make you happy. Instead of walking away, will you stay and trust God to fill the empty places in your life? He is the only one that can provide the happiness you are seeking. And the way He provides it is sometimes surprising.

Both of us (Steve and Alice) have experienced traumatic, heartbreaking struggles and have found that our times of suffering were the catalysts God used to help us discover intimacy with Christ. Like you, in the midst of difficulties, we just wanted to find a way out of them, but Jesus wanted us to find peace in the midst of them. The only way we could do that was by drawing closer to Him.[3]

The same is true for you. Even in those times when your prayers seem to go unanswered, if you wait patiently, He will give you a peace that protects your heart and provides a happiness that is more wonderful than you can imagine.[4]

Anne Graham Lotz, daughter of Billy Graham, writes these words about one of the storms in her life:

These storms of suffering have increased and intensified in my life because Jesus wanted me
    to soar higher in my relationship with Him—
      to fall deeper in love with Him,
        to grow stronger in my faith in Him,
          to be more consistent in my walk with Him,

to bear more fruit in my service to Him,
to draw closer to His heart,
to keep my focus on His face,
to live for His glory alone![5]

When you live for God's glory, happiness isn't elusive.
It doesn't fade in and out like the tides, but is a constant
source coming from within.

In the Bible, God calls it joy.

Ten Scriptures For Meditation

1.

Those who wait on the LORD will find new strength.

ISAIAH 40:31

2.

"The LORD your God...will rejoice over you with great gladness.
With his love, he will calm all your fears."

ZEPHANIAH 3:17

3.

"Come to me, all of you who are weary
and carry heavy burdens, and I will give you rest."

MATTHEW 11:28

4.

Nothing...will ever be able to separate us from
the love of God that is revealed in Christ Jesus our Lord.

ROMANS 8:39

5.

"Everything is possible with God."

MARK 10:27

6.

"For I know the plans I have for you...
plans for good and not for disaster,
to give you a future and a hope."

JEREMIAH 29:11

7.

His peace will guard your hearts and minds
as you live in Christ Jesus.

PHILIPPIANS 4:7

8.

I can do everything with the help of Christ
who gives me the strength I need.

PHILIPPIANS 4:13

9.

May our Lord Jesus Christ and God our Father...
comfort your hearts and give you strength
in every good thing you do and say.

2 THESSALONIANS 2:16–17

10.

Give all your worries and cares to God,
for he cares about what happens to you.

1 PETER 5:7

God's Way to Happiness

The Bible has sometimes been referred to as God's
Handbook of Happiness, and studying it and meditating
on what it says is the only way to discover what God really
wants for us. Once you trust the Bible as the authority for

your life, you won't base your decisions on what other people think or on what feels good for the moment.

What do we find about happiness when we spend time in the Bible? For one thing, God uses words like *contentment, joy, comfort, fulfillment,* and *peace* more often than He uses *happiness.* And He never associates these wonderful words with actions that violate His commandments and principles. So, for example, since He considers marriage beautiful and sacred, turning away from your husband is not likely to bring the happiness God desires for you.

Does God want us to be happy? Yes. But it is not the happiness we might seek through self-fulfillment, and it is not the feeling that ebbs and flows with circumstances and possessions. God wants us to have the kind of happiness that endures—joy, peace, and contentment—and these only come through trusting Him, obeying Him, and loving Him, even when it's hard.

In his book *Sacred Marriage,* Gary Thomas develops an idea that we have found especially helpful when women ask us whether God wants them to be happy. He suggests that perhaps the purpose of marriage isn't to make us happy, but to make us holy.

Thomas suggests that marriage is more than a sacred covenant with another person. It is also a spiritual discipline designed to help us know God better, trust Him more fully, and love Him more deeply.[6] It might be a new concept to think of your marriage as a tool God uses to develop intimacy with Him. But we believe that if you embrace this

209

idea, it will revolutionize the way you think about your marriage. Your relationship then becomes a form of ministry—especially if your husband is unlovable. It is no longer about you and your happiness, but about God and what will bring Him glory.

This may sound like cold comfort when you first hear it. It may sound like God wants us to suffer. What it really means is that God wants us to grow, especially grow closer to Him, and He will use anything He can to accomplish that goal. In the meantime, if you accept the idea that happiness is not the main purpose of being married, you will be freed from a lot of disappointment and disillusionment. You will be set free to depend on God for your true happiness—a happiness that is not dependent on positive circumstances. It will be a happiness that is both internal and external, and no one can take it away from you.

Can God...

Can God soften my heart? *Yes!*

Can God bring back my love? *Yes!*

Can God change my husband? *Yes!*

Can God change me? *Yes!*

Can God make my husband more lovable? *Yes!*

Can God make me more lovable? *Yes!*

Can God make our marriage beautiful? *Yes!*

After reading an early version of this manuscript, one woman wrote to us and said:

> I still struggle with the idea of walking away or somehow totally changing my husband. We go through ups and downs, and I wouldn't be honest if I said our marriage was easy. It never has been, and until my husband totally surrenders to God, it never will be. (I sound like it's all his fault and I know it's not.) I just wanted you to know that I read your book as though it was written just to me. You clearly state the truth that God's purpose for us isn't to make us happy, but holy. I think this is key when a woman has closed her heart and is ready to walk away. I want to be happy, but that will only come through God and from His grace.

If you are struggling with an unhappy marriage, we hope this will be a helpful word for you as you stand at a crossroads in your marriage. You can choose one road that claims to lead to happiness but actually moves you away from God. Or you can choose a more difficult path that leads you closer to Him.

Before making your decision, ask yourself where the road will lead. Then spend some time praying about it. We hope you will choose the path that leads to life-changing and abundant joy.

Something to Try

You can choose just one...

- How would you describe the difference between happiness and joy? List three contrasting attributes of each.

  _____   _____

  _____   _____

  _____   _____

- Review the eight statements by Anne Graham Lotz on pages 206–7. Circle the ones you believe Jesus wants for you to experience during these difficult days in your marriage.

- Write several sentences describing how you feel about the quote by Gary Thomas at the beginning of this chapter: "What if God designed marriage to make us holy rather than to make us happy?"

- Select one of the ten Scriptures listed on pages 207–8. Write it out on a three-by-five card, and memorize it during the next few days. As you memorize, think about each word, and thank God for His amazing love and care for you.

Chapter 16

The *What If* Game

Consult not your fears, but your hopes and dreams.

POPE JOHN XXIII

ast week Christine reached a life-defining moment. She told me (Steve) it was like a burst of sunshine after long periods of heavy cloud cover. She and her husband, Monte, had worked through some of the biggest problems of their marriage, and they were finally dismantling the walls that had built up over the past four years. Instead of walking out, she had decided to stay.

But yesterday when Christine came to see me, she seemed confused and wasn't sure what she wanted to do. Monte hadn't reverted back into his sullen moods, and there hadn't been any big blowups. But for some reason Christine had started playing the "what-if game"—with nothing but negative playing pieces. Despite all the progress she and Monte have made and her belief that God wants her to stay in her marriage, all Christine could think about yesterday was, *What if Monte doesn't change? What if he starts ignoring me again? What if the hurt returns? What if I really would be happier if I left?* As a result of these what-ifs, fear had taken the place of hope, and Christine was wondering if she really wanted to keep trying.

Sticking Points

You might feel like Christine when it comes to your marriage. On certain days you believe that you and your husband can build a wonderful future together. On other days, you want to run away and never look back.

There are five common "what-ifs" that cause women to doubt their decision to stay in their marriage. Even one can keep you frustrated and floundering—and some women get hung up on all five! The good news is that once you confront and deal with them, the what-ifs lose their power. So let's take these popular sticking points and disarm them one at a time:

What if I can't trust him? When you married your husband, you gave him your heart, your body, and your dreams. And for one reason or another he betrayed that trust, trampled on your feelings, and took you for granted. You promised yourself that you would never let him get close to your heart again. And now, even though you may want to trust him, you find yourself holding back.

Trust is fragile because hurts take a long time to heal, but mistrust keeps you forever locked in the past. Instead of dwelling on your husband's previous behavior, try to get a clear view of what he is doing now. Can you see evidence that he is actually "getting it" and starting to change—or at

214

least trying to? If he is still consistently doing the very things that caused all your hurts and heartaches, then your doubt is justified. But if he seems serious about making changes, then try giving him another chance. Don't walk away just because change is hard and rebuilding trust takes time. Watch and wait a little longer to see what God can do—both in your husband's behavior and in your heart.

To Forgive

To forgive is to set a prisoner free
and discover that the prisoner was you.

To forgive is to reach back into your hurting past
and recreate it in your memory
so that you can begin again.

To forgive is to dance to the beat of God's forgiving heart.

To forgive is to ride the crest of love's strongest wave.

LEWIS B. SMEDES[1]

What if I can't forgive him? It is much easier to write about forgiveness than to do it, but we know from personal experience that it is the only way to move forward. Your husband cannot undo all the unbearable wrongs and foolish insensitivities, and they may have piled up so high that you can't even see past them. You are trapped in a room of pain and as difficult as forgiveness is, it is the only key that will unlock the door. Staying in that room with those awful memories will only multiply your hurt.

When you have been deeply hurt, forgiveness can seem like an endless process. You can think you have put all the hurts behind you only to have them overwhelm you again. You may go through the process outlined in chapter 7 more than once—and still have to do it again. And there may well be times when your sense of justice rebels at the idea of forgiving your husband for the pain he has caused you. Forgiving may feel like letting him get away with something terrible. Almost certainly, it will seem like something he doesn't deserve.

On those difficult days, when forgiveness seems not only hard, but also undesirable, we urge you to cry out to Jesus and ask Him to help you through. He understands more than anyone else what you are going through. How Jesus must treasure the sight of you trying to forgive in the same way He forgave you.[2]

It may help to keep in mind that forgiveness is not the same thing as forgetting. You can't simply turn off your memories by an act of the will. But you can choose to set the memories aside and move forward. Though it takes time, it really is possible. When you choose forgiveness, the vivid memories of what your husband has done will eventually fade into softer, less painful hues.

What if I can't let go of my anger? The longer you have dwelled on your husband's faults and selfish insensitivities, the angrier you have probably become. This lingering anger may be uncomfortable—and can be harmful—but it can also feel good because it gives you a sense of power over your husband. You may use your anger as your justification to ignore him, put him down, shut him out, yell in his face, or even to walk out on him.

Releasing your anger means giving up some of this power, and you may be reluctant to do that. You might be thinking things like, *He hurt me. Why can't I do the same back to him?* You want him to feel the loneliness, rejection, and neglect that you have felt. Or you may simply feel too vulnerable without your anger to let it go.

If your husband has shown that he is sincerely sorry for hurting you and has made some offer of restitution, it is time to move forward. Focusing on his effort for reconciliation rather than on what he did wrong will help you let go of the anger. But even if he doesn't have a humble heart about his wrongs, holding on to grudges and the desire for revenge will ultimately hurt you more than it hurts him. Holding on to anger can cast a long shadow on your life and paint your future with bitterness. At the very least, it keeps you glued to a dark past. Letting go of it releases you to a bright future.

How do you let go of your anger in a positive way? When anger first hits, many women find relief by *talking it out* or *journaling it out*. Others find that *working it out* through exercise or tending the garden brings release. Still others find creative outlets like *painting it out, quilting it out,* or *sculpting it out* are helpful. However, if your mind

217

and heart continue to struggle with letting go, you might need some sort of ritual to bring closure. Physically *crossing it out* by destroying reminders of your hurts, redesigning places where they happened, or writing the offenses down and burning the paper can be helpful to many. If you are truly struggling with letting it go, we suggest you go back to chapter 8 and read and follow the steps presented there. They really do work.

What if I don't want to change my mind? At this point, you may have spent a lot of time and courage to get to the point where you are ready to walk out. Maybe you have figured out a plan and even shared it with sympathetic friends. There is a certain comfort and security in having done this, and the idea of changing your mind seems like a giant, embarrassing step backward.

Perhaps, deep in your heart, you don't want to see your marriage improve. Even when your husband starts doing the very things you always wanted him to do, you may resent the fact it took him this long or that you had to work so hard to finally get him to care about the fact that your relationship was on the skids. Your thoughts and desires may already be somewhere else, and even if your husband begins to make progress toward becoming the man you have prayed for him to be, it may feel like too little, too late.

All these feelings are understandable, but do you really want to base a major life decision on pride, resentment, and stubbornness? When you refuse to at least consider a change of mind, you may well be hardening your heart toward God as well as to your husband, and we know you don't really want that. Keeping a soft heart and an open attitude does not mean you are a pushover or that you can be easily fooled. It means you want to hear God's voice and be sensitive to His touch. A soft heart opens the way for you to discover the great dreams God has planned for your future.[3]

What if I don't want to let go of my newfound freedom? If you've made plans to walk out (or have actually left), you may be experiencing a sense of relief and freedom. Being removed from the challenges, frustrations, and work of your marriage probably feels good. You like being able to do whatever you want, whenever you want, and with whomever you want—not having to clear your plans with your husband or to even care about how he feels or what he might say.

At some point in most marriages, the idea of this kind of freedom sounds good to every wife—and to every husband as well. But as many walk-out women soon discover, new fantasies can crumble as quickly as the old ones did. What adult, single or married, actually gets to do whatever she wants? Chances are, what looks like freedom now will soon be full of new problems—along with regret and sadness for all you have left behind.

Every tomorrow has two handles.
We can take hold of it by the handle of anxiety,
or by the handle of faith.

HENRY WARD BEECHER

Depending on God

For Christians, the solution to all the "what-ifs" of life depends on asking God for guidance and help. When we are obedient to Him, we never have to look forward with fear or backward with regret. But even this may be problematic if you are weary from struggling and trying to improve your marriage. You may know all the verses about what God wants for you, but you are so disappointed by your marriage that you just don't care. Maybe you've reached the point where you don't *want* to depend on God anymore. You're not all that interested in doing what He wants. You may have half decided to walk away from God as well as your husband.

It's not that you plan to stay away from God forever, but right now you may feel angry and let down. You may feel awkward with other Christians, and going to church may trigger emotions of guilt and alienation. Even praying may seem worthless and hollow because part of you doesn't want to hear God's voice. What if God asks you to change? What if He asks you to forgive? What if He asks you to stay in your marriage?

If we were sitting beside you right now, we hope you would sense the deep compassion we have for you. You would also understand that we care too much about you, your husband, and your family to just let you go. With all the urgency we can pour onto a printed page, we are pleading with you to open your heart to God and hear what He has to say to you about your marriage. We especially urge you to lean on His comfort and His wisdom—because you've never needed your heavenly Father more than now.

If you are not reading the Bible on a regular basis, we suggest you begin today by reading the Psalms. Many of the Psalms start with the writer being stuck in emotional despair, but as he journals his way through his difficulties, the psalmist arrives at the place where he can trust God no matter what he is facing. Try reading one or two psalms every day, and ask God to show you ways to depend on Him to remind you of the many ways He can heal and renew you. One of our favorites is Psalm 40, which promises that God will hear your cry, put a new song in your heart, and show you His compassion and lovingkindness. It ends with the assurance that God will truly be your help and deliverer.

A New Set of What-Ifs

In Martha Bolton's book *Still the One* we discovered a wonderful list of what-ifs.[4] As you ponder the answers to these questions, it is our prayer that you will use them to replace the doubting, negative "what-ifs" you have been dwelling on:

What If...

...the grass isn't greener on the other side of the condominium complex?

...you discover that the kids aren't better off without
you?

...you're throwing away something that's irreplaceable?

...you can never get it back?

...you didn't leave?

...you gave it one more chance?

...you fell in love all over again?

...this time things truly were different?

...you made it?

Something to Try

You can choose just one...

- Of the five what-ifs listed on pages 214–9, which one(s) plague your thoughts the most? Using Martha Bolton's list on the previous page as an example, try to reverse your negative what-ifs to positive ones.

- Have you been unable to forgive your husband for something? What do you need him to do to help you forgive him? Set aside some time this week to discuss this together.

- Has your husband been unable to forgive you for something? What does he need you to do to help him forgive you?

- In his book *The Five Love Languages*,[5] Gary Chapman lists five actions that help people feel loved:

  - Words of affirmation
  - Quality time
  - Gifts
  - Acts of service
  - Physical touching

  Discuss with your husband which one of these most communicates love to you. Ask him which one most communicates love to him. Then consider how you might say "I love you" in *his* love language sometime in the next forty-eight hours.

Chapter 17

Dreaming New Dreams

*Diamonds cannot be polished without friction
nor our human lives perfected without trials.*

AUTHOR UNKNOWN

ven if you have been thinking about walking out on your marriage, the fact that you are reading this chapter indicates that there is still promise for you and your husband. If you have followed up with your commitment to pray for your husband daily and read these chapters with the support of a trusted friend, you should already be seeing some progress—or at least some insight into what is wrong with your marriage.

You're probably also aware of how much is left to do. Your marriage still seems far removed from what you dreamed of long ago. Instead of waltzing gracefully around the dance floor, your husband's steps—and perhaps your own—are still awkward and stumbling. Yet you have opened your heart and listened carefully—and we hope you still hear music playing. If you will take the risk to turn toward your husband and keep dancing, we believe you'll find that the dance goes more smoothly with time. Despite all your trials and troubles—or even because of them—you can finally start moving together with a flow you didn't think possible.

Yes, there are still wounds from the past, but they can be healed in time. And yes, there will be missteps, as Karla Downing writes in *10 Lifesaving Principles for Women in Difficult Marriages:* "Your husband isn't going to be everything you want him to be, and you aren't going to be everything he would like you to be. When you reach the point of accepting each other as imperfect people who will sometimes disappoint, it brings healing to both."[1]

Healing is a wondrous word, and it can happen if you will make a fresh start, walk by faith, and pray constantly that your marriage will become all God wants it to be.

A New Commitment

Can you flip back through the pages of time and remember the holy and life-binding vows you made on your wedding day? You made them not only to each other, but also to God. Even if you wrote your own words, it is likely that you made promises of sacrificial love and faithfulness to one another. You guaranteed that no matter what, you would always be together.

Perhaps you did not understand exactly what you were promising on that memorable day. With all the excitement, you were probably only looking at the dream side of your romance. After all, you expected your love to become more beautiful and more precious. You expected it to grow deeper, stronger, and closer. Instead, you grew apart. Now it is time to come back together and renew your commitment.

A Vow

If things get better for us, I will love you.
If things get worse, I will love you.
If we get rich beyond our wildest dreams, I will love you.
If we grow poorer and don't own much, I will love you.
If you get sick, I will love you.
If you remain healthy, I will love you.
…No matter what happens, I will always love you.

GARY AND BARBARA ROSBERG[2]

227

If you have followed our suggestions on working through this book, you have been praying for your husband on a regular basis. We now ask you to pray for your marriage as you have never prayed before. Ask God to increase your affection toward your husband and to increase your husband's affection toward you. Thank God for every good quality your husband has and for every sweet memory you have shared. Plead with God to deliver you from any unforgivingness or bitterness you still hold in your heart. Allow God to give you beauty for ashes. Invite Him to become the center of your life and the Lord of your marriage.

And then, as soon as possible, we'd like you to take another step—to come together and renew your sacred vows to one another.

Right now the task of restoring those commitments might seem overwhelming or like a waste of time. You may be too weary to even think about it, or you resist the idea because you still have doubts about how everything will work out. Even if you have fears, there comes a time when you must step out in pure faith. You won't be alone. You will have the prayers and support of all who hold marriage sacred, and Jesus can be trusted to strengthen you.[3]

Renewing your vows doesn't have to be a big occasion—though it can be. But whether you do it at a romantic hideaway with just you and your husband or during a celebration with friends and family, make it a special time. Tenderly hold hands, look deeply into each other's eyes, and ask God to strengthen your resolve to remain devoted to one another.

As you and your husband plan what you will express to each other, try to include all ten of the following ideas:

We Commit To…

- *Oneness:* We will cling to one another in body, soul, and spirit.

- *Affirmation:* We will speak the truth in love, seeking to encourage each other in all we say.

- *Togetherness:* We will set aside quality time for just the two of us to enjoy romance, laughter, listening, sharing, and companionship.

- *Prioritizing:* We will put each other above everything else in our lives except for God.

228

℗ *Nurturing:* We will actively nurture and improve our relationship by attending seminars, by studying marriage books, by seeking out mentors, and by discovering other resources that will help our marriage get better.

℗ *Faithfulness:* We will not hurt our relationship by engaging in activities that could lead to physical or emotional intimacy outside of our marriage.

℗ *Honesty:* We will not lie, deceive one another, or keep secrets from each other.

℗ *Protection:* We will physically, financially, emotionally, socially, and spiritually protect each other.

℗ *Fellowship:* We will become involved in a good church or group where we can find friends who value marriage and family.

℗ *Endurance:* We will take seriously our promise to love and cherish one another for all the days of our lives "until death do us part."

Dreaming New Dreams

After you renew your vows, spend time dreaming some new dreams for your future together. Maybe you want to plan a second honeymoon, find a significant ministry you can do side by side, or look ahead to a time when you can move to a little cottage in the country. Whatever you decide, take the first steps now toward making your dreams come true. Have dream conversations often—very often—

for there is a powerful bonding when you share common goals and aspirations. Your ability to stay together during the roughest problems is greatly influenced by the dreams you build during the good times.

We are excited about your future! Love that endures through difficulties can become deeper, wider, purer, and more beautiful than you could ever imagine. You have been in our hearts and prayers during all the months that we were writing this book, and we will continue to pray and dream with you. We are trying to imagine you and your husband years from now. We see you even more devoted to each other than when you first fell in love.

An unknown author wrote the following sweet story. We dedicate it to you as a tribute to your enduring love:

> Can there be anything more beautiful than young love? Yes, there is a more beautiful thing. It is the spectacle of an old man and an old woman finishing their journey together. Their hands are gnarled, but still clasped; their faces are seamed, but still radiant; their hearts are physically bowed and tired, but still strong with love and devotion for one another.
>
> Yes, there is a more beautiful thing than young love. Old love.[4]

Something to Try

You can choose just one...

- If you and your husband could rewrite and renew your vows, knowing that you both would keep the promises, what would you both want to include? What would you hesitate to include? (Does that tell you anything about the areas of your marriage that still need work?)

- Discuss with your husband the ten commitments on pages 228–9. Circle the ones you want to work on during the next year. Hold hands and commit to one another as many of them as you truthfully can at this point in your marriage.

- On your next wedding anniversary, consider renewing your marriage vows. Ask a pastor to officiate, and invite your family and closest friends. Celebrate with confetti and balloons!

- We would enjoy hearing from you. Please take a moment to drop us a note c/o Multnomah Publishers, P.O. Box 1720, Sisters, Oregon, 97759. If you would like to schedule a speaking engagement, see contact information at our website: www.thewornoutwoman.com.

- Keep dreaming new dreams—always!

Coming Alongside:
A Guide for Meeting Together

A man was walking in a wilderness.
He became lost and was unable to find his way out.
Another man met him. "Sir, I am lost, can you show me
the way out of this wilderness?" "No," said the stranger,
"I cannot show you the way out of the wilderness,
but maybe if I walk with you, we can find it together."

EMERY NESTER[1]

a t the beginning of this book, we asked readers to commit to meeting regularly with a pastor or a trusted friend for a period of three months as they work through some of the issues that led them to consider walking out on their marriages. This brief guide is designed to facilitate those meetings and provide a structure for discussion.

For the purpose of this guide, we suggest you meet weekly for about an hour in a place that is comfortable for both of you. Because there are seventeen chapters and only thirteen weeks in a three-month period, you will need to make a decision about how to address this. Whether you choose to cover more than one chapter on some weeks, meet more often than once a week, continue getting together for a longer period, or pick and choose among the most relevant chapters is up to you—and something to decide in your first meeting together.

The guide for each meeting contains questions for the two of you to discuss and a "homework" assignment for the person you are helping to work on between sessions. (Reading the next chapter in the book is always part of the homework for both of you.) Keep in mind that these meetings are not intended to take the place of professional therapy—and the "helper" does not need counseling credentials. The point is to be a source of encouraging support and honest feedback to help the potential walk-out woman explore her feelings and understand her options.

A Word to the Walk-Out Woman

The fundamental message of this entire book is *don't give up hope*—and we pray this process of meeting together will help you rediscover hope for your marriage. Even if you are inwardly convinced that these meetings won't make any difference in your decisions, we ask that you put that thought away for the duration of your times together. Try to keep an open mind even if your heart is clenched shut, and trust God to work in your life as you give Him this chance.

A Word to the Helper

It is quite wonderful that you are willing to walk alongside someone who is going through difficult times. We are aware that balancing compassion and encouragement with wise counsel can be a challenging task, but we also believe that what you are doing can make a monumental difference in another person's life. And you don't have to be a professional to do this. All it really takes is a desire to serve and a commitment to both honesty and hope. Whether you are a pastor, a peer counselor, or a concerned friend, we trust the following suggestions will help you.

During your times together, try to build a sense of relationship. The woman you are meeting with needs to know that you genuinely care and are genuinely listening. Sometimes as we listen, we can get so focused on how we are going to respond that we aren't hearing the other person's hurts, fears, and frustrations. But often the simple act of listening can be an instrument of God's grace.

However, listening doesn't mean you have to say nothing—or agree with everything the woman you are meeting with says. It's important to counterbalance her frustration and negativity with reminders of the positive aspects of her marriage and husband. As you do so, try to instill notes of hope.

In addition, although emotions need to be listened to and validated, they can lead to dangerous choices. A potential walk-out woman is often making emotional decisions without thinking through the full consequences—and when you see this happening, it's certainly appropriate to say so. Feel free to share your own experiences and the lessons you have learned from them. Don't be afraid to share your honest opinion—but always in the context of your concern for her and a full awareness of the hurt that has driven her to seek your counsel.

In all you say, strive to speak the truth in love. The fastest way to shut another person down is with an insensitive or judgmental attitude. Pat answers run a close second.

Above all, try to be patient. You might feel the need to say something profound that triggers an "aha" experience—and an immediate recommitment to the marriage. But women who have arrived at the point of walking out have come through a series of injuries and emotional struggles, so the journey to healing and reconciliation will probably take time. As we mentioned in chapter 9, it is important to realize that change rarely happens in giant, life-rattling leaps. Usually it occurs in small, unsteady steps—often a few steps forward, and then some back. One of your roles as a helper is to point out progress during those forward steps and provide support and encouragement during times of stumbling backward.

In all of this, we believe prayer is one of your most powerful tools. We encourage you to spend time in prayer between sessions, offering up the process to God and asking for wisdom and guidance. In addition, if the woman you are meeting with agrees, we recommend that you pray together briefly at the beginning and end of each of your times together. We have found that whatever a person's belief system, she almost always appreciates heartfelt prayer.

We genuinely value people like you who are willing to take the time and effort to come alongside others. It is our prayer that God will truly bless you and the ones you are trying to help.

A Guide for Meeting Together

Prologue: White Linen and Candlelight

The purpose of your first visit is to get acquainted and lay a foundation of trust and understanding for future sessions. The following questions will help accomplish this.

Discussion Ideas

1. If you had been at the banquet described in this prologue and had the opportunity to talk privately for five minutes with Dr. Steve, what would you have said about your marriage?

2. Discuss what you need to hear from your husband that will give you hope that your marriage really can survive.

3. Review the first three items in the "Something to Try" section on page 21. Choose at least one of these that you feel comfortable discussing during your first time together—and spend some time talking about it.

Assignment

Select a journal, a blank book, or just a fresh legal pad in which to record your thoughts about the whole process of working on your marriage. This week, write down some of your highs and lows as they occur during the week. Right before your next meeting, look back over what you have written.

Chapter 1: What's Going On?

Discussion Ideas

1. Talk about your highs and lows from the previous week. Can you see any patterns in what happened? What triggered the high points? What triggered the low points?

2. If you haven't already done so, fill out the "walk-out symptoms" checklist on pages 26–8, and score your list as directed. Did you score higher or lower than expected? Did the frequency at which you experience some of the symptoms surprise you—or did reading about any of them hit you hard emotionally? Why do you think you had this response?

3. Discuss your feelings about meeting together. What are your anxieties or excitement about meeting with someone for the purpose of working on your marriage? Do you feel it is worth the effort? (If either of you feels reluctant about this process, review the following Scripture verses: Proverbs 12:15; 15:22; 19:20.)

Assignment

Refer to the passage from Isaiah 61:1–3 quoted on page 29. Imagine what it would be like for God to touch your marriage in such a way that you have beauty for ashes…the oil of joy for mourning…and a garment of praise rather than the spirit of heaviness. Think about what your marriage would look like after God has touched it in these ways.

Chapter 2: Lost Dreams

Discussion Ideas

1. Spend some time brainstorming about where you formed your expectations for marriage. Consider sources like family of origin, peers, novels, television, church, and seminars.

2. Besides your marriage, what are some of the greatest disappointments you have experienced in your life? How have these disappointments affected you? What have you done to try to work through or overcome these disappointments?

3. What are some of the ways your husband has disappointed you? How have you disappointed him?

Assignment

Write out different ways you have tried to communicate to your husband the disappointments you are feeling.

Chapter 3: He Doesn't Get It

Discussion Ideas

1. Discuss together the results of last week's assignment.

2. In what ways are men like buffalo and women like butterflies? Do you think this accurately depicts the ways you and your husband communicate? What other metaphors might describe the differences between men and women? Between you and your husband?

3. In which three specific areas do you feel your husband doesn't understand your needs? Within these three areas, what do you wish he could understand about your thoughts and feelings? What have you done recently that has been most effective in getting your husband to understand the pain you are feeling? What has been the most ineffective?

4. Discuss how you can best share the following four things with your husband:

   • What you need from him

   • How you need it

   • When you need it

   • Why you need it

Note: Don't overwhelm him by dumping all your needs on him at once. It's best not to share too much at a time.

5. Look together at the sidebar on page 54 (about what husbands and wives should pay attention to). Discuss the sidebar and then circle three items in the "wives pay attention" list that you are willing to focus on during the next week.

Assignment

As you focus on the items you have circled in the "wives pay attention" sidebar, jot down some of the ways your husband responds to your attentiveness. Also, notice how doing these things makes you feel.

Chapter 4: What Happened to the Good Times?

Discussion Ideas

1. Discuss the results of last week's homework assignment. How did you feel when you specifically paid attention to your husband?

2. Describe some of the best or most treasured "souvenirs" of your heart that are related to your marriage. (Consider such memories as how you met, when you first fell in love, how he proposed, your wedding, honeymoon, favorite vacations, children's birthday parties, etc.)

3. Of the five vulnerable times of marriage listed on pages 63–5, discuss which ones you think are most difficult and why. What are some strategies that could help couples get through these times? Which of these apply specifically to you and your marriage?

Assignment

Think of one activity or tradition for your marriage that you would like to start in the next few months. Write down details and the first step to making it happen.

Chapter 5: Keeping Score

Discussion Ideas

1. Discuss last week's homework assignment. Have you mentioned to your husband the activity or

tradition you would like to start with him? If so, what was his response? If you didn't mention it to him—why didn't you?

2. Review the idea of a personal love bank as described in this chapter, and think back over how you and your husband have gotten along the past few days. How would you describe the balance in your love bank? Check one and discuss:

❑ More full than empty

❑ In need of some regular deposits

❑ Barely on the positive side

❑ One more withdrawal will change it to negative

❑ Overdrawn but hoping for a deposit

❑ Has had a negative balance for some time

❑ Bankrupt

3. How do you think your husband would describe the balance in his love bank? (If he is still in denial, you may have to add the category "Full and overflowing.")

4. Discuss what it means to "grade with grace," as explained in this chapter. If your love bank has been overdrawn for some time, how would it feel to give your husband a fresh start? If you find yourself resisting the idea, discuss why it would be so difficult.

Assignment

Choose at least one of the items from "Something to Try" on page 79. Come prepared next week to discuss what you did.

Chapter 6: The Downside of Divorce

Discussion Ideas

1. When have you come closest to considering a divorce from your husband? What were your most compelling reasons? What has kept you from taking the step up to now?

2. Of the "reasons for regret" listed in this chapter, which ones do you consider the most compelling? Which ones fail to convince you? What causes you to feel this way?

3. If you left your marriage today, what "baggage" are you most likely to carry to your next relationship? (Everyone has some!)

4. Role-play how you would counsel someone else who was considering divorce. (Note: In your role-playing, avoid the four *A*s: abandonment, addictions, abuse, and adultery.)

Assignment

Divide a sheet of paper lengthwise under the headings "reasons to go" and "reasons to stay." Using this chapter as a guide, list as many reasons on each side as you can think of. Be as honest as you can, and be sure to bring the list with you to the next meeting.

Chapter 7: It Hurts So Much

Discussion Ideas

1. Discuss the list you made as part of your homework assignment. How did it feel to actually put some of these items down on paper? (Put this list aside for now, and plan to review/revise it when you finish working through this book— we predict some of your feelings will change.)

2. What hurts from your husband do you have trouble forgiving or forgetting? What did he do last week that hurt you the most? How have any of these hurts affected your trust, dreams, appreciation, libido, and love?

3. Look over the following list together. Identify which items your husband would need to do or experience before you could forgive him.

   - Apologize

   - Feel remorse

   - Make restitution

   - Change his ways

   - Allow you time to "get over it"

   - Recommit to the marriage

   - Suffer consequences

   - Get right with God

244

4. Look over the list again, and ask which actions you think your husband would want you to do or experience before he could forgive you for the ways you have hurt him.

Assignment

During the next week, work on at least one of the actions from the above list that you must take in order for your husband to forgive you for a recent offense.

Chapter 8: I'm So Mad I Could...

Discussion Ideas

1. Read Ephesians 4:26 and brainstorm together how people can express anger without sinning. How do these ideas relate to the last time you were angry with your husband?

2. When have you been most angry with your husband? What made you feel that way? How did you respond? How long did your anger last? What effects did it have on your relationship and your general sense of well-being?

3. How do other people know when you're angry? Discuss which "warning signs of anger" on page 109 you show most often. What additional symptoms do you have?

4. Do you derive any benefits from anger in your relationship? Does it help you get your way or

give you energy to confront problems? How could you handle your anger differently but still keep some of these benefits?

Assignment

Anger is often a secondary emotion—which means there is another emotion beneath it. During the next week, pay attention to the emotions beneath your anger. From the following list, try to identify what emotion triggered the angry response:

Hurt	Powerlessness
Fear	Disappointment
Embarrassment	Guilt
Anxiety	Discouragement

Chapter 9: This Lady Has the Blues

Discussion Ideas

1. According to one theory, unexpressed or unacknowledged anger can turn to depression. Have your ever "stuffed" or ignored your anger for so long that you became depressed?

2. Explore your history of depression by discussing the following questions:

℠ Did either of your parents struggle with **depression**?

℠ When was the first time you remember feeling depressed?

℠ How frequently have you felt "blue" over the last six months?

℠ Describe your darkest episode of depression.

3. Do you believe that "the blues" are an issue in your life right now? Discuss why you think this is or is not true. (If feelings of depression are severe or long-lasting, please consider making an appointment with your primary care physician or a professional counselor. If there has ever been a time when you have taken antidepressants, this is one indicator that you may need to seek additional help.)

4. Describe the statements you tend to make to yourself about your marriage, your family, your friends, your personal attributes, and life in general. Discuss how this self-talk affects the way you think or feel on a daily basis.

Assignment

Based on how your discussion time went, choose one of the following:

1. Review the social, active, fun, and health categories listed on pages 124–5. Do at least one activity in *each* category during the next week.

2. Try to think of a woman you know who struggles with depression. Review the categories listed on pages 124–5, and consider how you might encourage her to do something uplifting.

Chapter 10: Different Walls

Discussion Ideas

1. Follow up on last week's assignment by describing in detail what you did and how your efforts affected your mood.

2. Discuss what the opening poem in this chapter says to you. How does it make you feel? How does it relate to your own marriage or affect your thinking about it?

3. How would you describe the methods you use to construct walls in your own marriage?

4. Review the five strategies for dismantling walls that begin on page 139. Brainstorm together how you can take the first steps to dismantle any walls you have been building in your marriage.

Assignment

Talk to your husband about the walls in your marriage. How strong or high are they? Who built them and why? (Note: Many men dislike this sort of conversation, and your husband may feel trapped and uncomfortable if you suggest it—especially if your attitude is critical or accusatory. Make sure to take your share of the responsibility for causing and building walls.)

Chapter 11: Let's Talk

Discussion Ideas

1. Discuss together how last week's assignment went—and especially how you and your husband were able to communicate about the issue of wall building. Did you experience any communication barriers that you believe are typical for your marriage?

2. Discuss together what you would like the communication in your marriage to be like. Be as specific as possible.

3. Reminisce about the best conversation you have had with your husband in the past month. What made it so good? If there haven't been any "good" conversations, try role-playing how you could successfully engage your husband in conversation. (Be as brief and nonthreatening as possible.)

4. Work together to identify the top areas of unresolved conflict in your marriage. Brainstorm potential resolutions to these issues using the three strategies outlined in the sidebar on page 156.

Assignment

This week, work on being "quick to listen, slow to speak" (James 1:19). Listen deeply to your husband's words, emotions, concerns, and even his nonverbal language.

Chapter 12: Reconnecting

Discussion Ideas

1. List some topics and activities both you and your husband are interested in or have enjoyed in the past. (If you believe you have none, then dig a little deeper—there is bound to be something. For example, consider what you enjoyed doing together when you were dating.) Discuss what you can do during the next week to build on these interests.

2. Talk about a practical task you and your husband can do together. How might you initiate such a project?

3. Since a couple's sexual relationship can have a profound effect on other aspects of connecting, explore how you feel about this aspect of your relationship. How do you believe your husband feels about it? (You don't really have to go into the details of your love life with your helper. The purpose of this discussion is to open the door for honest and healthy discussion with your husband. But if you or your helper feels uncomfortable with this kind of discussion, or if there appear to be deep difficulties in this aspect of your marriage, consulting a professional might be a wise step.)

Assignment

Ask your husband on a date, and do something you both consider fun. Make a big deal of it and have a great time.

Chapter 13: Take Care of Yourself

Discussion Ideas

1. Discuss how your date with your husband went. What did you do? Where did you go? How did you both feel about your time together?

2. Of the six basic needs listed on page 176, which ones do you feel are currently being adequately met in your life? Which ones need attention? Brainstorm the beginning steps for taking better care of yourself in at least one of these deficient areas.

3. What responsibilities have you taken on during the past year that you wish you had said no to? Discuss why you added them to your schedule. Explore whether your saying yes involved people pleasing, a need for affirmation, perfectionist tendencies, or being a bit of a control freak.

Assignment

Try the exercise described in chapter 12 under the topic "Caring Days." Pick at least two days during this week when you go out of your way to do something on your husband's "makes me feel loved" list.

Chapter 14: The Fantasy of Something Better

Discussion Ideas

1. Back in chapter 2, you discussed what factors influenced your expectations about marriage. Return to that topic now, but this time discuss what may be *currently* causing you to fantasize about something better for your marriage. (Consider: male models or actors that build false expectations, "male bashing" that portrays men in a negative light, women's magazines that give a narrow view of a perfect relationship, the marriage of a friend who leaves you envious, or an emotional connection with someone outside your marriage.)

2. How are you responding to your fantasies? (Possibilities: talking about them with friends, dwelling on them, or even making plans to act them out.) In what ways are these thoughts tempting you to action? If you are considering an affair or already involved in one, be sure to bring this to the discussion!

3. Discuss the five fatal fallacies in the sidebar on page 194. These are really excuses you may give yourself for indulging in harmful or dangerous behavior. Which of these have you heard yourself saying or thinking? Which do you think are the most dangerous?

4. Discuss together the Thomas Kinkade quote on pages 193–4. What things do you dream of doing that you could actually do with your husband?

Assignment

Beginning tomorrow, start writing down as many examples as possible of ways God has blessed you during your life. Add to the list daily and bring it with you next week.

Chapter 15: Doesn't God Want Me to Be Happy?

Discussion Ideas

1. Look together at the "blessing list" you prepared as part of last week's assignment. If you could only come up with a few items, brainstorm some more. You might try coming up with ideas for each letter of the alphabet.

2. At what times in your life have you felt closest to God? What helped you feel that close? What challenges have you faced in your lifetime that drew you closer to Him?

3. Talk about why God would be more concerned with your holiness than your happiness. What do you think about applying that idea to your marriage?

253

Assignment

Meditate on Galatians 5:22–23, which teaches that if the Holy Spirit controls our lives, He will produce this kind of fruit in us:

  ❧ Love   ❧ Goodness

  ❧ Faithfulness ❧ Peace

- Patience   - Joy

- Kindness   - Self-control

- Gentleness

How would each of these qualities improve your marriage and your life in general?

Chapter 16: The *What If* Game

Discussion Ideas

1. What kinds of what-ifs do you tend to worry about the most?

2. Talk together about the issue of trust. Who has broken trust with you in the past? How do you think those experiences have affected your relationships? What helped you regain trust? What might be the first step in regaining trust with your husband?

3. If you have already made preliminary plans to walk out, you may not want to give up the freedom you are anticipating. What are some ways you could experience more freedom within the context of your marriage? (Ideas could include developing a hobby, getting away with girlfriends, going back to school, developing career options, or volunteering where you have a passion.)

Assignment

Talk to your husband about something you can dream about together with the goal of bringing it to reality sometime in the next twelve months. If you are not yet in a place in your relationship where you feel comfortable doing this, write out a list of dreams you might like to share with your husband when you are ready.

Chapter 17: Dreaming New Dreams

Discussion Ideas

1. After getting together for this many weeks, you have probably built a very positive relationship— and remaining faithful to your meeting times is an important milestone for you. Find some way to make this time fun—by enjoying refreshments, going out to lunch, taking a walk together, or even exchanging gifts.

2. Discuss what have been some of the highlights of your times together. Which meetings were the most positive, powerful, or life changing?

3. If you and your husband should decide to renew your marriage vows, what are some ways you could make that event memorable and meaningful? Discuss some ideas for location, guests, content, etc.

4. Discuss the ten areas of recommitment beginning on page 228. Which ones still feel scary? Which ones feel uplifting and exciting? (They might be the same ones!) Which areas does your husband struggle with? Which do you believe he would be most enthusiastic about?

5. Discuss whether or not you will keep meeting together either on a regular or occasional basis. If you are not going to continue, review together what you need to keep doing to help yourself and your marriage.

Assignment

Sit down with your journal or a piece of paper, and consider where you are now in your commitment to your marriage. Make a list of three specific steps you can take in the next month to "walk on" in your marriage rather than "walking out." If appropriate, start making plans now for renewing your marriage vows.

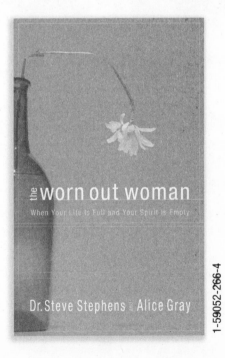

Life-Changing Advice in a Quick-to-Read Format!

With sales of over 700,000 copies, the Lists to Live By series has something for everyone—guidance, inspiration, humor, family, love, health, and home. These books are perfect gifts for all occasions.

For the Moments
That Matter Most

From the compilers of the popular Lists to Live By series come 200 powerful lists by some of the industry's top Christian speakers and authors. The lists are divided into thirteen easy-to-reference sections, with topics like virtue, prayer, faith, marriage, God and His Word, worship and praise, community, eternal hope, and family. Full of humor, insight, and practical advice, these lists will deepen faith, strengthen relationships, nurture hope, and build character.

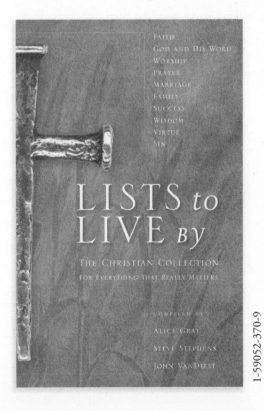

FAITH
GOD AND HIS WORD
WORSHIP
PRAYER
MARRIAGE
FAMILY
SUCCESS
WISDOM
VIRTUE
SIN

LISTS to
LIVE By

THE CHRISTIAN COLLECTION
FOR EVERYTHING THAT REALLY MATTERS

COMPILED BY
ALICE GRAY
STEVE STEPHENS
JOHN VANDIEST

1-59052-370-9

www.multnomahbooks.com | www.alicegray.com

Recommended Reading

For More Information

The books in this section cover a wide range of subjects such as communication, intimacy, making it through the tough times, rediscovering love, and answers for the tough questions. All of them have powerful ideas that will not only help your marriage survive, but also become wonderful again.

Arp, David and Claudia Arp. *10 Great Dates to Revitalize Your Marriage*. Grand Rapids, MI: Zondervan, 1997.

Bolton, Martha. *Still the One: Keeping the Love, Keeping the Laughter*. Grand Rapids, MI: Revell, 2001.

Chapman, Gary. *The Five Love Languages: How to Express Heartfelt Commitment to Your Mate*. Chicago, IL: Northfield, 1992, 1995.

Clarke, David. *A Marriage After God's Own Heart*. Sisters, OR: Multnomah, 2001.

Cobb, Nancy, and Connie Grigsby. *How to Get Your Husband to Talk to You*. Sisters, OR: Multnomah, 2001.

Dobson, James. *Love Must Be Tough: New Hope for Marriages in Crisis*. Sisters, OR: Multnomah, 2004.

Dobson, James, and Shirley Dobson. *Night Light: A Devotional for Couples*. Sisters, OR: Multnomah, 2000.

Farrel, Bill, and Pam Farrel. *Men Are Like Waffles, Women Are Like Spaghetti*. Eugene, OR: Harvest House, 2001.

Gottman, John. *Why Marriages Succeed or Fail: And How You Can Make Yours Last.* New York: Simon & Schuster, 1994.

Graham, Ruth Bell. *Never Let It End: Poems of a Lifelong Love.* Grand Rapids, MI: Baker, 2001.

Gray, Alice, Steve Stephens, and John Van Diest. *Lists to Live By for Every Married Couple.* Sisters, OR: Multnomah, 2001.

Harley, Willard F. Jr. *His Needs, Her Needs: Building an Affair-Proof Marriage.* Tarrytown, NY: Revell, 1986.

Harley, Willard F. Jr., and Jennifer Harley Chalmers. *Surviving an Affair.* Grand Rapids, MI: Revell, 1998.

Janssen, Al. *The Marriage Masterpiece: A Bold New Vision for Your Marriage.* Wheaton, IL: Tyndale, 2001.

Kalmbach, Deb, and Heather Kopp. *Because I Said Forever: Embracing Hope in a Not-So-Perfect Marriage.* Sisters, OR: Multnomah, 2001.

Lynch, Chuck. *You Can Work It Out: The Power of Personal Responsibility in Restoring Relationships.* Nashville, TN: Word, 1999.

McGinnis, Alan Loy. *The Friendship Factor: How to Get Closer to the People You Care For.* Minneapolis, MN: Augsburg Fortress, 1979.

Parrott, Les, and Leslie Parrott. *The Love List: Eight Little Things That Make a Big Difference in Your Marriage.* Grand Rapids, MI: Zondervan, 2002.

Parrott, Les, and Leslie Parrott. *When Bad Things Happen to Good Marriages: How to Stay Together When Life Pulls You Apart.* Grand Rapids, MI: Zondervan, 2001.

Rainey, Dennis. *Lonely Husbands, Lonely Wives: Rekindling Intimacy in Every Marriage.* Dallas, TX: Word, 1989.

Rosberg, Gary, and Barbara Rosberg. *Divorce Proof Your Marriage.* Wheaton, IL: Tyndale, 2002.

Smalley, Gary, with John Trent. *Love Is a Decision*. New York: Pocket Books, 1989.

Smith, Debra White. *Romancing Your Husband: Enjoying a Passionate Life Together*. Eugene, OR: Harvest House, 2002.

Stephens, Steve. *20 Surprisingly Simple Rules and Tools for a Great Marriage*. Wheaton, IL: Tyndale, 2003.

TerKeurst, Lysa. *Capture His Heart: Becoming the Godly Wife Your Husband Desires*. Chicago, IL: Moody, 2002.

Thomas, Gary. *Sacred Marriage: What If God Designed Marriage to Make Us Holy More Than to Make Us Happy?* Grand Rapids, MI: Zondervan, 2002.

Waite, Linda J., and Maggie Gallagher. *The Case for Marriage: Why Married People Are Happier, Healthier, and Better Off Financially*. New York: Doubleday, 2000.

Wheat, Ed. *Love Life for Every Married Couple: How to Fall in Love, Stay in Love, Rekindle Your Love*. Grand Rapids, MI: Zondervan, 1980.

Promises and Prayer

Scripture promises and prayer are two essentials that help us through life's most difficult problems. There are so many wonderful resources available from Christian publishers that it was almost impossible to select only a few. Here are some of our favorites that are especially meaningful when your marriage is hurting.

Arthur, Kay. *Lord, Teach Me to Pray in 28 Days*. Eugene, OR: Harvest House, 1982.

Barnes, Bob, and Emilie Barnes. *Minute Meditations on Prayer*. Eugene, OR: Harvest House, 2003.

Brownlow, LeRoy. *A Psalm in My Heart*. Fort Worth, TX:

Brownlow, 1989.

Cymbala, Jim. *Breakthrough Prayer: The Secret of Receiving What You Need from God.* Grand Rapids, MI: Zondervan, 2003.

Fuller, Cheri. *When Couples Pray: The Little-Known Secret to Lifelong Happiness in Marriage.* Sisters, OR: Multnomah, 2001.

Gibbs, Terri, comp. *God's Promises Day by Day.* Nashville, TN: Countryman, 2003.

Gothard, Bill. *The Power of Crying Out: When Prayer Becomes Mighty.* Sisters, OR: Multnomah, 2002.

Kopp, Heather. *God's Little Book of Guarantees for Marriage.* Sisters, OR: Multnomah, 2002.

Myers, Ruth. *31 Days of Praise: Enjoying God Anew.* Sisters, OR: Multnomah, 1994.

Omartian, Stormie. *The Power of a Praying Wife.* Eugene, OR: Harvest House, 1997.

Wales, Susan, with Holly Halverson. *Standing on the Promises: A Woman's Guide for Surviving the Storms of Life.* Sisters, OR: Multnomah Publishers, 2001.

Notes

Prologue: White Linen and Candlelight

1. Ruth Bell Graham, *Never Let It End: Poems of a Lifelong Love* (Grand Rapids, MI: Baker, 2001), 33.

Chapter 1: What's Going On?

1. Ruth Harms Calkin, *Love Is So Much More, Lord: A Celebration of Marriage* (Cook, 1979).
2. Isaiah 61:1–3, NKJV.
3. Sometimes it is difficult to find a good counselor in the area where you live, or perhaps you just cannot afford the expense. In these situations, try locating a trained lay counselor or check out audio- or videotapes on the subject. The recommended reading list in this book can direct you to some of these. In addition, Focus on the Family in Colorado Springs, Colorado (1-800-AFAMILY), offers a referral service as well as print, audio, and video resources.

Chapter 2: Lost Dreams

1. Quoted in Tim Gardner, "Great Expectations," *Marriage Partnership* 15, no. 1 (spring 1998): 46.
2. Ephesians 5:25, *The Message*.
3. Ruth Bell Graham, *Never Let It End: Poems of a Lifelong Love* (Grand Rapids, MI: Baker, 2001), 7.
4. Quoted in Les Parrott and Leslie Parrott, *When Bad Things Happen to Good Marriages: How to Stay Together When Life Pulls You Apart* (Grand Rapids, MI: Zondervan, 2001), 33.

Chapter 3: He Doesn't Get It

1. Nancy Cobb and Connie Grigsby, *How to Get Your Husband to Talk to You* (Sisters, OR: Multnomah, 2001), 159.

Chapter 4: What Happened to the Good Times?

1. Thomas Kinkade and Nanette Kinkade, *The Many Loves of Marriage* (Sisters, OR: Multnomah, 2002), 103.

2. Matthew 12:34, NASB.

3. Adapted from Linda S. Mintle, "Marriage Myths" *Christianity Today* 23, no. 6 (Nov/Dec 2001): 2001. Article based on Linda S. Mintle, *Divorce Proofing Your Marriage: 10 Lies That Lead to Divorce and 10 Truths That Will Stop It* (Lake Mary, FL: Siloam, 2001).

4. Phillip C. McGraw, *Relationship Rescue* (New York: Hyperion, 2000), 194.

Chapter 5: Keeping Score

1. Willard F. Harley Jr., *His Needs, Her Needs: Building an Affair-Proof Marriage* (Tarrytown, NY: Revell, 1986), 16.

2. Condensed from Alice Gray, Steve Stephens, and John Van Diest, comp., *Lists to Live By for Every Married Couple* (Sisters, OR: Multnomah, 2001), 110.

3. Proverbs 11:27.

Chapter 6: The Downside of Divorce

1. Linda J. Waite and Maggie Gallagher, *The Case for Marriage: Why Married People are Happier, Healthier, and Better Off Financially* (New York: Doubleday, 2001), quoted in Jim Killam, "The Case for Marriage," *Marriage Partnership* 18, no. 1 (spring 2001): 38.

2. Ibid., 38.

3. Alice Gray, Steve Stephens, and John Van Diest, comp., *Lists to Live By for Every Married Couple* (Sisters, OR: Multnomah, 2001), 69.

4. Patrick F. Fagen and Robert E. Rector, "The Effects of Divorce on America," Backgrounder #1373 (Washington, DC: The Heritage Foundation), 5 June 2000.

5. David Popenoe, "Debunking the Divorce Myths," The National Marriage Project at Rutgers University, *Discovery Health Channel* website, 2002, http://health.discovery.com/centers/love relationships/articles/divorce.html (accessed 23 February 2004).

6. *Woman's Day*, 5 August 2003, 156.

7. Gary Chapman, *The Five Love Languages* (Chicago: Northfield Publishing, 1992, 1995), 133.

8. Malachi 2:16.

9. Ecclesiastes 3:11.

10. Proverbs 13:22.

Chapter 7: It Hurts So Much

1. Judy Gordon, quoted in Alice Gray, comp., *A Gift of Comfort for a Hurting Heart* (Sisters, OR: Multnomah, 2002), 61.

2. Psalm 55:4, 6–8, NIV.

3. James Dobson and Shirley Dobson, *Night Light: A Devotional for Couples* (Sisters, OR: Multnomah, 2000), 275.

4. Ephesians 4:32, NASB.

5. Condensed from chapter 13 of Steve Stephens and Alice Gray, *Worn Out Woman: When Your Life Is Full and Your Spirit Is Empty* (Sisters, OR: Multnomah, 2004), 155–64.

Chapter 8: I'm So Mad I Could...

1. Gary Smalley with John Trent, *Love Is a Decision* (New York: Pocket Books, 1989), 90.

2. Some of the ideas in this list are from Nicole Johnson, *Fresh-Brewed Life* (Nashville: Thomas Nelson, 1999), 107.

3. Ephesians 4:26–27, NASB.

4. John Gottman, *Why Marriages Succeed or Fail* (New York: Simon & Schuster), 72–97.

5. Johnson, *Fresh-Brewed Life,* 98.

6. Proverbs 15:1.

7. Adapted from Smalley with Trent, *Love Is a Decision,* 92–3.

8. Reader tip in *Woman's Day,* 1 September 2003, 16.

Chapter 9: This Lady Has the Blues

1. Cheryl K. Ewings, "When Depression Hits Home," *Today's Christian Woman* 21, no. 6 (November/December 1999): 90.

2. Romans 5:3–4.

3. Luke 11:25–26.

4. Philippians 4:8.
5. Numbers 6:24–26.

Chapter 10: Different Walls

1. Richard A. McCray, "Walls," © 1998. Used by permission.
2. Selected from Steve Stephens, *Marriage: Experience the Best* (Gresham, OR: Vision House, 1995).
3. Psalm 46:1–3.
4. Al Gray and Alice Gray, comp., *Stories for a Man's Heart* (Sisters, OR: Multnomah, 1999), 63. This German legend, grounded in history, was first written down by the Brothers Grimm. We found it in a newspaper column called "Insights" written by Rochelle M. Pennington of Campbellsport, Wisconsin.

Chapter 11: Let's Talk

1. Willard F. Harley Jr., *His Needs, Her Needs: Building an Affair-Proof Marriage* (Tarrytown, NY: Revell, 1986), 10.
2. Ann Landers column quoted in Ed Wheat, *Love Life for Every Married Couple* (Grand Rapids, MI: Zondervan, 1980), 106.
3. Thomas Kinkade and Nanette Kinkade, *The Many Loves of Marriage* (Sisters, OR: Multnomah, 2002), 100.
4. Ephesians 4:29, NIV.
5. This list is adapted from Steve Stephens, *Marriage: Experience the Best* (Gresham, OR: Vision House, 1995), 93–121.
6. Charles M. Sell, *Achieving the Impossible: Intimate Marriage* (Portland, OR: Multnomah, 1982), 66.
7. Steve Stephens, *20 Surprisingly Simple Rules and Tools for a Great Marriage* (Wheaton, IL: Tyndale, 2003), 69–70.
8. Ibid., 70.

Chapter 12: Reconnecting

1. Condensed and retold from a story originally written by Daphna Renan, found in James Dobson and Shirley Dobson, *Night Light: A Devotional for Couples* (Sisters, OR: Multnomah, 2000), 106–7.

2. Willard F. Harley Jr., *His Needs, Her Needs: Building an Affair-Proof Marriage* (Tarrytown, NY: Revell, 1986), 78–83.

3. Lysa TerKeurst, *Capture Her Heart: Becoming the Godly Husband Your Wife Desires* (Chicago: Moody, 2002), 114.

4. Ibid., 59.

5. This idea was adapted from an exercise originally developed by Richard B. Stuart in his book *Helping Couples Change: A Social Learning Approach to Marital Therapy* (New York: Guilford Press, 1980), 197–207.

6. The idea of the jars was adapted from TerKeurst, *Capture His Heart,* 78–9.

Chapter 13: Take Care of Yourself

1. Isaiah 40:11, NIV.

2. Selected from Kim Thomas, *Even God Rested* (Eugene, OR: Harvest House, 2003), 99–100.

3. Reader tip in *Woman's Day,* 7 October 2003, 15.

Chapter 14: The Fantasy of Something Better

1. Thomas Kinkade and Nanette Kinkade, *The Many Loves of Marriage* (Sisters, OR: Multnomah, 2002), 61.

2. Quoted in Cindy Crosby, "Why Affairs Happen," *Marriage Partnership* 18, no. 1 (spring 2001): 30.

3. Kinkade and Kinkade, *The Many Loves of Marriage,* 58–9.

4. Robert Jeffress, *The Solomon Secrets* (Colorado Springs: Waterbrook, 2002), 107–17.

5. Matthew 5:27–28.

6. Dennis Rainey, *Lonely Husbands, Lonely Wives* (Dallas: Word, 1989), 83.

7. Adapted from Willard Harley Jr. and Jennifer Harley Chalmers, *Surviving an Affair* (Grand Rapids, MI: Revell, 1998).

Chapter 15: Doesn't God Want Me to Be Happy?

1. Psalm 16:11, NIV, emphasis added.

2. Jeremiah 31:3.

3. John 16:33.

4. Philippians 4:7.
5. Anne Graham Lotz, *Just Give Me Jesus* (Nashville: Word, 2000), 200.
6. Gary Thomas, *Sacred Marriage* (Grand Rapids, MI: Zondervan, 2000), back cover.

Chapter 16: The What If Game

1. Selected from Lewis B. Smedes, "Forgiveness—The Power to Change the Past," *Christianity Today,* 7 January 1983. http://www.christianitytoday.com/ct/2002/149/55.0.html (accessed 8 March 2004).
2. Ephesians 4:32.
3. Jeremiah 29:11.
4. Condensed from Martha Bolton, *Still the One* (Grand Rapids, MI: Revell, 2001).
5. Gary Chapman, *The Five Love Languages* (Chicago: Northfield Publishing, 1992, 1995), 119.

Chapter 17: Dreaming New Dreams

1. Karla Downing, *10 Lifesaving Principles for Women in Difficult Marriages* (Kansas City, MO: Beacon Hill, 2003), 156.
2. Gary Rosberg and Barbara Rosberg, *Serving Love* (Wheaton, IL: Tyndale, 2003), 18.
3. Philippians 4:13.
4. Selected from Alice Gray, comp., *Stories for the Romantic Heart* (Sisters, OR: Multnomah, 2002), 41–2.

Coming Alongside: A Guide for Meeting Together

1. Quoted in Don Baker and Emery Nester, *Depression: Finding Hope and Meaning in Life's Darkest Shadow* (Portland, OR: Multnomah, 1983), 37.